I0469803

Drop Shipping

The Ultimate Guide To Generating $10,000/Month In Passive Income With Drop Shipping And Online Marketing Platforms

Author: Ralf Percy

Free Gift

This book includes a bonus booklet. This giveaway may be for a limited time only. All information on how you can secure your gift right now can be found at the end of this book.

Table of Contents

These 14 New Habits Will Double Your Income, from Today

An Easy Cheat Sheet to Adopting 14 Powerful Success Habits:

Stop Procrastinating and Start Earning with Intent Now!

Are Your Bad Habits Keeping You from the Life You Want?

Mine definitely were, but then I dedicated myself to new habits

– and everything changed!

Most people get stuck in same old routines. We eat the same breakfast, we talk to the same people. Human beings are creatures of habit, and it locks us into negative cycles we don't even know are there. Like me, you've had enough of the same-old, same-old. It's time for change!

This guide gives you the 14 most high impact habits that helped me double my income nearly instantly, when I set out on this journey. I will help you change, and I'll make it stick!

Drop Shipping

This FREE Cheat Sheet contains:

- Daily success habits that the most successful people in the world live by

- Common, but little-known habits that will surprise you

- Details on what Stephen Covey, Oprah Winfrey, Elon Musk, Bill Gates and Albert Einstein did that you aren't doing to maximize your earning potential

- Tips on how to overcome habit fatigue

- The reality of adopting difficult, challenging habits and the rewards that result

Scroll below and click the link to claim **your cheat sheet!**

It's tough to admit that you're doing it wrong. I went through it, and it sucks. After that I was free to change however necessary, to meet my goals. I want you to know that change is waiting for you. This guide is so easy to follow, and if you put it to work in your life – you will double your income.

Adopt these habits, and change your life.

CLICK HERE!!

Book Description:

Are you itching to sell products, but don't want to go through the hassle of keeping them in stock? Drop shipping is one of the best ways to make money online, and this is how you get started.

Everyone wants to be in drop shipping! But there is a lot of misinformation floating around on how to make it work. Save yourself time, money and effort when you invest in a guide that orientates you with a logical, systematic strategy. You'll go from 0 to $10,000 a month in just a couple of months.

In *Drop Shipping*, I take a closer look at getting the basics right; then I lay a solid foundation on top of that with proven strategic plays. From setup to picking the right sales channels, creating your supply chain and marketing the goods – this is how you create a shop that sells on the internet.

In this useful guide you'll learn:

- To get the basics of drop shipping right for smooth sailing

- The incredible benefits of drop shipping as a business model

- To spot the disadvantages that creep in as you build your business

- How to conduct critical market research

- How to find the right product and set up your company

Drop Shipping

- The A-Z of the drop shipping procedure and how to market products

If you're a talented marketer and want to make real money selling things online, drop shipping is a superb starting point. Many millionaires got their start with this fast, easy online model.

Invest in a guide that teaches you exactly what it takes to make it in the turbulent world of drop shipping. This is the knowledge that will take your income to the next level!

Learn how to become a drop shipper with this guide.

Get the guide and start your business!

Introduction

Drop shipping is a method of fulfilling orders. It is not a business model, and "drop shipper" is not specifically a job title. As a drop shipper, you are considered an e-commerce entrepreneur, a store owner, more or less, and of course, a content creator.

The normal process of running a retail shop is that you pay high amounts of rent for a location, stock your shelves with great products, advertise yourself to locals, and hope that the business rolls in. This brick-and-mortar approach has been dying out for small business owners over the last couple of decades, and you're probably aware that the cost of rent is going up regardless of the economy's ups and downs. The traditional e-commerce setup removes the overhead of rent and allows you to make sales around the world, but you still have to purchase and stock products in your home, a warehouse space, or a storage unit. Then, there is the method of using a fulfillment service that accepts your products and handles the shipping process for you once sales are placed. This method has greatly saved people time, but it still requires a lot of overhead. The drop shipping fulfillment method is a little different.

With drop shipping, you work directly with suppliers. You list the products that they sell on your website, or through third-party selling platforms, and when the order is placed, you send them the information. From there, they handle the shipments on your behalf. Much like having your inventory shipped by a fulfillment service, you still have to deal with any customer service issues that arise. Also, it is your job to create the website and content that will draw in customers, and ultimately make the sales possible. Once drop shipping is set up, this is basically how the process works:

- You locate products from your supplier.

- Write content and create a system for customers to be able to purchase.

- Accept payment from customers.

- Place an order with the supplier (sometimes semi-automated, or it may require you to place the order yourself, depending on the suppliers you are working with).

- Supplier ships directly to the customer on your behalf, netting you a small profit from a product you've NEVER touched.

- You handle any customer concerns that may arise afterward.

This book comes with a FREE Bonus chapter section as a gift. You can download them for free. The free content can be found at the bottom of this book.

Chapter 1
Basics of Drop Shipping

Before we get into developing your understanding of how to grow your profits on the web, it's important that you understand what drop shipping is. This chapter is going to talk about what the dropshipping supply chain is so that you fully understand where you fall in this supply chain as someone interested in drop shipping yourself. As you're going to see after reading this chapter, there is great profit to be had within the dropshipping supply chain, as long as you know where to position yourself and your business. Now, let's look at the components of a drop shipping supply chain.

Dropshipping Entity 1: The Creator of the Product

Also known as the manufacturer, the first entity involved in a drop shipping supply chain is the person or company that creates the product in the hopes of generating a profit by selling it. Even though manufacturers are likely to offer great deals on their products, they usually only do this in bulk. Typically, a manufacturer is going to sell to what's known as a vendor or wholesaler, because they know that these types of companies will be able to sell large amounts of their product quickly. Unless you already have a ton of money and know that the product is going to sell well on the internet, purchasing from the manufacturer is not the best idea for an aspiring small-business owner such as yourself, as it's unlikely that you have the space to hold this much inventory at one time.

Dropshipping Entity 2: The Vendor

After the manufacturer, the next drop shipping supply entity is known as the vendor. The vendor is the point in the supply chain that will sell the products that the manufacturer has made to large retail stores to make a profit. In order to make a profit, the vendor will need to raise the price of the product when they sell it to a retail store. However, it is still not recommended that you look at your drop shipping business as capable of competing at the vendor level, at least not at the beginning. The amount of product that these vendors can sell is quite large, and many times these vendors will even have contracts with the companies that they're selling to. Unless you already have contacts that will be able to get you these types of deals, being a vendor is also not in your best interest.

Dropshipping Entity 3: The Seller

Since you're most likely not going to be the manufacturer or the vendor, your business will likely fit best within the seller portion of the supply chain. The seller can best be described as an individual or small business who purchases the product from the vendor. The seller makes a profit by ensuring that the price at which they're selling the product to their customers is higher than the price they bought it for. This is an important concept to understand in regard to developing an online drop shipping business, because if you end up selling your products at a price that is similar to or lower than the price at which you bought the product yourself, making a profit will be nearly impossible. Typically, you want to sell your products at 1.5 or 1.6 percent the price that you bought it for. Of course, you can adjust this percentage according to your business.

Beware of Fees

In addition to communication being a pillar of a reliable drop shipping business, it's also important to point out from the onset that any manufacturer or vendor that tries to charge you a fee to drop ship with them should not be trusted. Many legitimate companies will drop ship products for you without needing to pay a fee. This may change as drop shipping becomes more popular, but for now, if you do find a company that is trying to charge you a fee in order to dropship, look elsewhere. If the product niche that you choose is incredibly small, you might be stuck dealing with companies that charge a fee, but for a majority of product markets, you should be able to find other companies that will provide you with their services for free. Don't be scared to shop around before choosing who you're going to buy your products from.

You Don't Need to Develop Your Own Product

The last important point is that when you create a drop shipping company for yourself, you're able to bypass the actual creation of the product. Instead, you're able to reap profit from companies that already manufacture these products. This is a big reason why drop shipping has become so popular recently. If you don't actually have to think of a product to create, why would you? Learning how to drop ship is thus an exciting alternative to what can otherwise be an incredibly stressful and time-consuming process. Of course, that's not to say that developing a drop shipping business isn't sometimes a stressful endeavor, but it is arguably less arduous than completely developing a new product from scratch.

This chapter has looked at the basics of drop shipping and has included details on what drop shipping is and how a drop shipping supply chain works. Understanding the basic components of traditional drop shipping will allow you to feel more comfortable when you enter the market. Even though online drop shipping has made it easier than ever before to start a business, the basics of drop shipping are still largely physical, rather than digital in nature.

In other words, if you don't use Shopify or Amazon FBA in order to drop ship, you're going to need to pick up the telephone and physically speak with someone from the manufacturer or vending company. I understand that talking on the phone seems so outdated, but with drop shipping, you may have to negotiate this way. Even if you use Amazon FBA or Shopify, you may still find that talking on the phone with the manufacturer will allow you to develop relationships with the company that you would otherwise be unable to cultivate. To be successful with drop shipping, it will be easier for you to integrate old methods of drop shipping with newer digital methods.

Drop Shipping is Not Just a Product-Focused Business

Because the customer is going to go through your drop shipping business, it essentially means that they do not have to interact with a large and sometimes-overwhelmingly slow manufacturer. This positions the drop shipper as a business that simply serves as a point of contact for a customer so that they do not have to go through the manufacturer or vendor themselves. With this being the case, it's important to understand that any drop shipping business is a service, rather than an operation that simply buys and re-sells products. Without good customer service, even a reputable drop shipping service is likely to go out of business. It's extremely important to keep this in mind because excellent client communication is key to any good drop shipping business.

Negotiating with Manufacturers, Vendors, and Other Sellers

As you can see from the description of each aspect of the supply chain above, as a drop shipping entity, you are mostly going to exist within the selling portion of the supply chain model. However, this does not mean that the potential does not exist for you to interact with all three of these drop shipping entities in some manner. A key aspect of any drop shipping business is figuring out which manufacturers and vendors will agree to ship their products to your customers on your behalf. In other words, instead of having a manufacturer or a vendor ship their products to you so that you can then ship to your customer, some manufacturers and vendors will agree to ship to other people for you, free of charge.

Chapter 2
Benefits of Drop Shipping

Drop shipping is a fast-growing industry because of its many benefits. Here are a few examples:

1. Less Capital

As stated in the first chapter, drop shipping companies do not need to handle and store inventory for their business. Therefore, a drop shipping business does not require huge amounts of capital. This is the biggest advantage of this kind of business model because it does not require the outflow of money just to buy inventory.

Traditionally, business owners needed to spend thousands of dollars on inventory before jump-starting their business. With drop shipping, these business owners can put their money into something else aside from inventory, like the development of a professional website.

2. Purchase upon making a sale

With drop shipping, merchants only need to purchase inventory whenever they make a sale to their customers. This means that a business owner does not even have to spend his own money to buy inventory. It is actually possible to start this business with very little money because the customers will technically be the ones paying for the inventory from the suppliers.

3. Easy to Start

Anyone can start a drop shipping company from the comfort of their home. Aside from the very small amount of money needed to start a drop shipping business, this business model is easy to start. All you have to do is find a reliable supplier with a great product that can be sold to the market. The key here is to know who to do business with and what products to sell.

4. Low Business Risk

With a drop shipping company, there is a significantly lower business risk. Since you do not need to spend thousands of dollars in inventory, you will not be stuck with a lot of unsold inventory if the business does not succeed.

Have you ever watched the Pursuit of Happiness? Will Smith's character was very optimistic about his new business venture. However, since his product was not in demand in the medical industry, he had trouble selling it. Also, he bought the entire inventory beforehand. So, when he could not sell his goods, he ran out of money which could have been used for other essentials. With drop shipping, you will not have to worry about getting into a similar situation.

5. Low Overhead

Aside from low capital requirement, you will no longer need to spend much on overhead because you will not need to manage loads of inventory. In fact, a huge number of drop shipping companies are actually managed by owners through their homes, simply with the use of a laptop. Drop shippers that work from home end up spending roughly $100 a month on overhead.

Obviously, the amount of overhead will eventually grow as your company grows, but this is relatively lower compared to other brick and mortar or traditional business models.

6. Wide Array of Products

When it comes to what you want to sell in your drop shipping business, the sky is the limit. You can actually sell a wide variety of products because you do not have to pre-purchase all of them for resale. As long as your supplier has a particular item in stock, you can list that up in your inventory for your customers. In a sense, you are just going to be an extremely effective intermediary for the supplier.

7. Flexible Area Location

You can start your own drop shipping company anywhere you want, as long as you have an internet connection. You can even just set up your laptop next to your bed and start working without even getting out of your pajamas. As long as you find reliable suppliers and you can communicate with customers easily, you can successfully manage this type of business.

8. Easy Work Scale

With drop shipping, business owners can easily scale their workload because the dropshipping suppliers will do most of the leveraging. You will only need to take in customer orders, and suppliers will bear all the additional processes needed to fulfill that particular order. Hence, you can actually expand your business with very little incremental work.

However, you will have to do customer service work, like dealing with customer disputes, but keep in mind that this kind of problem can be avoided if you personally know your suppliers as well as the quality of products that they provide.

These are only a few of the most common reasons why this type of business model is growing. All of these benefits make drop shipping very attractive to business people. However, this does not mean that drop shipping does not come with a price. In the next chapter, we will look at the disadvantages of drop shipping.

Chapter 3
Disadvantages of the Drop Shipping Model

Drop shipping does come with some downsides. Like any business, there are always positive and negative situations, and you need to decide what will work best for you.

- Low Income – you may not need a lot to start up the business, but you also have low margins or income. The key to using drop shipping to run a home-based company is to sell a large number of goods at extremely low prices. Let's consider the manufacturer acting as a drop shipper. The manufacturer wants to sell as many goods as possible, so the company is going to sell to retail locations as well as to multiple wholesalers who disperse the goods as a drop shipper. The retail locations may sell as a drop shipper, on the internet, and have a land-based business. As an example, look up a hedgehog duvet. Now, go to Amazon and type in Newrara 3D Hedgehog bedding white with Hedgehog digital 4pcs duvet cover set. Look at the price difference for the same duvet set. Beddinginn is a UK company. Newrara is selling using Amazon, and they ship the product. You have two companies selling the exact same product. One or more parties can sell nearly anything you find through a drop shipper, and in fact, is often sold by hundreds of people. With drop shipping, you must provide a low-profit-margin for yourself to beat the competition.

- Inventory Concerns – you are not in charge of the inventory. The drop shipper is, and sometimes, they do not quickly alert you of what items are in or out of stock. Therefore, it is important to sync your website inventory with the suppliers and to ensure that everything listed on your site is not out of stock.

- Shipping – shipping can be a little complex as the drop shipper is sending out the goods. If your customer orders three items, they may ship from three different manufacturers. If you charge $3.99 per item for shipping, the customer is going to think you are overcharging. You want to provide affordable shipping that is only charged once, not individually, so this can hurt your bottom line. You may not make any profit on the sale if your prices do not account for the multiple shipping charges.

- Supplier Errors – you must take responsibility and apologize for errors made by the supplier because the customer believes you are in charge of the entire order. The customer does not understand that you may not have anything to do with the quality or missing items due to botched shipments or low-quality packing. Therefore, it is important to choose drop shippers with high reputations and avoid those that have complaints.

People that make money using drop shipping create a model that best suits their target audience. We currently live in a world where a person will order a product at a slightly higher cost to avoid the shipping fee. Also, people look around and assess multiple sites to see who has the best overall cost. An example of this business model is the sale of used books online.

Drop Shipping

The most successful home-based businesses that use drop shippers are those who are run by a person who examines the items they are going to sell for quality, personally speaks with the drop shipper, read reviews about him, and understands the power of marketing quality products

A Short message from the Author:

Hey, are you enjoying the book? I'd love to hear your thoughts!

Many readers do not know how hard reviews are to come by, and how much they help an author.

I would be incredibly grateful if you could take just 60 seconds to write a brief review on Amazon, even if it's just a few sentences!

>> Click here to leave a quick review

https://www.amazon.com/review/create-review?asin=XXXXXXXXX

Thank you for taking the time to share your thoughts!

Your review will genuinely make a difference for me and help gain exposure for my work.

Chapter 4
Conducting Important
Market Research

As an entrepreneur, throughout your journey, you will be conducting market research in many ways. This is something that will occur at almost every level of your business, and skipping it in the initial steps is perhaps one of the easiest ways to set yourself up for failure. As we continue, we are going to talk about many types of market research, and while we have dedicated this chapter to research, we will continue to speak about this throughout the whole process.

Choosing a Niche

If you are familiar at all with the world of online marketing or e-commerce, you have probably heard the term "niche" come up quite a lot. A niche can simply be described as a product or content category, but it can be very specific or very broad. It is important to understand that a broad niche may open the door for a lot of products, but a narrow niche is much easier to market. This is because the market isn't usually as saturated with sellers, so there is less competition.

The ideal niche selection is one with a relatively high amount of consumers that are looking for these types of products and a relatively low amount of competition. This is difficult to find, so many of us are going to work in niches where we believe the competition is moderate and where we can provide something they can't.

Of course, as a drop shipper, you are free to start more than one store and tackle more niches as you grow your business. However, at the start, it's advised to pick one niche and stick to it.

You can try several methods to pick a niche:

- Consider what you love. If there is a market for it, selling something you are passionate about can make the job much more enjoyable, especially as you're still waiting to turn in a significant profit. To help you with this, make a list of things you love.

- Consider what those around you love. Many people don't draw inspiration from those around them. If all of your friends are crazy about compression socks, there might be something there! Add some of these items to your list.

- Consider the common problems of a demographic you believe you can market products to, then consider the types of products that might help them solve these problems. Add these to your list.

- Think of any other ideas that may be viable and under-represented. The longer your initial list, the better chance you have to find a profitable niche.

With this list in hand, you will now have to conduct some research to determine which of these niches may be viable. If you're lucky, you'll be left with a handful of options, and you may be able to choose the one that best fits your personal interests. If you're unlikely, you'll find a lot of dead ends and have to go back to the drawing board. Do not give up until you have found a viable niche.

Start with keyword research. The best way to start eliminating choices from your list is to start by understanding how this niche is represented on Google's Keyword Planner. The Keyword Planner is a tool that gives us data to help us create paid advertisements with Adwords, but it also gives us a general idea of how often any word or phrase is being searched, if people are spending a lot of money advertising those specific words, and it also helps us find other related words and phrases. When choosing a niche, what we're really looking for is keywords that have high amounts of searches per month and a relatively low competition rating. If the original term you enter into the search bar doesn't have a lot of data, but a very similar word does, it is safe to say you simply picked a lackluster keyword. That doesn't mean the niche itself is lackluster!

Remove niches with low amounts of searches or high amounts of competition. Personally, I only try to work on niches or keywords that have 10,000 searches at the very least and low to moderate competition. It is better to have more searches and lesser competition. Write out the competition and amount of searches besides words that aren't crossed off your list, because you're still not done considering which niche you want to be in. If you've crossed off everything by now, it's time to come up with more niches and start over.

Consider the products available in this niche. This can be done in a few ways. The easiest place to start is Amazon or eBay, but you may also want to look at what is available in wholesale marketplaces like AliExpress.com or Alibaba.com. What you are looking for is two things. First, you want to look at how much the product is selling for, and second, how popular is the product? Select a small handful of products for the niche you are considering and determine these two factors.

In terms of a product's popularity, you can use Amazon as your benchmark. This is done by looking at the sales ranking shown on the product pages, usually near the bottom. The lower this sales ranking number, the more viable and popular a product is. As a general rule of thumb, never bother with products that are ranked lower than 100,000. Are these products and similar products selling regularly? If they are, it may be a viable niche.

Take note of the pricing on Amazon as well, as their prices are a good gauge for the retail price you may charge. However, if you're working through your own online store, you may charge a slightly higher price. From there, try to locate these items or similar items on websites like Aliexpress or Alibaba. Later, you may be able to check with other suppliers, but as a beginner, if you hope to get started selling soon, you will likely be working with one of these websites for your first handful of products. As you note down these prices, you can purchase these products, and this will help you determine if the price you are buying for allows enough profit. In e-commerce, as a general rule, we try to buy products for a third of the cost that we can sell them for. Because we aren't actually shipping anything ourselves, we will be able to stretch that rule a bit, and this happens quite often.

As you learn more about sourcing products and the many other details of running your drop shipping business, it will become easier to determine how pricing works with your niche selections. For now, just make sure that products are selling and available for reasonably less than the retail price. With drop shipping, it is common to sell for a bit higher than the lowest prices found on websites like Amazon. That may seem counterintuitive, but if you're handling your marketing and customer service well, you will be surprised to see that you can sell for higher prices than you might have expected.

If the most obvious products aren't popular or cannot be purchased at prices that will allow for a decent profit, it may be time to cross that particular niche idea off your list and try the next one. Once again, if none of your niche ideas are working out, it is important to return to the beginning of the niche selection process. It has happened to me several times, but when I did land on a niche that ticked off all the boxes, it was well worth my efforts.

In the end, you will hopefully have a few options and an idea of which niche options are the best for your purposes. Having a niche means that you can focus on a product area, and this helps significantly with marketing and in understanding the demographic that makes up your customer base. Keep in mind that if you decide to stick to a particular niche, it's important to you actually stick to it. For your first store, it is wise to stick to this particular niche. Once you have established your first niche, you can always start a second online store and expand.

Not Choosing a Niche

For some drop shippers, there's just no reason to choose a niche. This only really applies if you're planning to sell through third-party marketplaces. For many, this decision may be easy as you do not really need to deal with much marketing, content creation, or social media interaction with potential customers. The upside is that there is a lot less work involved and you can focus on releasing any products that seem viable rather than just focusing on a specific category.

The downside is that using a third-party marketplace means that you are going to make less per sale, so you need to make a much larger amount of sales to earn the same amount that a dedicated online store earns selling the same products. There's no reason you can't use this method of selling every decent product you can find while still focusing on your main niche in more depth. I believe that a well-created store with excellent marketing is going to bring in a lot more profit. However, it is also a lot more work and investment, so you have to decide what matters most to your bottom line.

Essentially, there is no reason to start your own dedicated online store if you're not going to focus on a niche. A store without a niche is like trying to recreate Walmart or another major retailer, which you simply can't do from the ground up, without a lot of money and helping hands. Your aim isn't to compete with these types of stores!

More About Keyword Research and Why You Should Care

Now that we've taken the time to consider niches with keyword research and a handful of other methods, let's backtrack a little and go back to the subject of keywords and keyword research. Keywords are the basis for how the internet is navigated; even paid advertisements are set up with the use of keywords. Therefore, you really need to understand that keyword research is going to be something that follows you throughout many parts of your e-commerce business. This includes:

- Determining if a potential niche is viable, as discussed before.

- Helping product pages become visible to common searches

within third-party marketplaces and search engines.

- Purchasing ads that display during relevant searches or appear for the appropriate audiences on social media websites.

- Drawing organic traffic to your website, blog, or other online content.

- Improving your overall search engine optimization.

As you can see, basically everything other than sending, receiving e-mails, and responding to comments on social media can be affected by keywords. In the end, you will need to utilize keywords throughout your website, product descriptions, and any other online content.

When it comes to keywords, as a general rule of thumb, we want to implement them in a very organic or natural way. The use of articles stuffed with keywords used to be a popular way to boost SEO, but as Google evolved, it has changed its search engine optimization considerations and the way it processes keywords. For a 500-word blog, your keyword should not be displayed more than 5 times. At the end of the day, though, when we're talking about content, the most important thing is for it to be great. Lackluster content with keywords may potentially help your ranking on Google, but it will do nothing for you once the potential customer leaves because your site is filled with low-quality content. When you have great content, keyword placement becomes less of a concern.

The major misconception about keyword usage is that people think they need to keep the keyword exactly how they found it when they conducted their original research. However, this isn't necessary.

Google doesn't differentiate between "best blow horns 2017" and "best blow horns in 2017." Small articles (the, and, but, for, that) between different keywords are of no great concern.

Implementing a keyword into your website name and the domain name is a good way to improve your overall search engine optimization slightly. This is especially true for the domain name. If I want to sell blow horns, "blowhorns.com" is the best possible domain name, and from there, other variations such as "blowhornstore.com."

When conducting keyword research, try to put together a huge list of keywords that will be viable for you, and when you are handling a new product, always go back to keyword research. For any text that is going to be online, you should take your time to focus on keyword research.

When working on Amazon, these things aren't as important, but again, we highly suggest starting your own store, blog, and marketing plan if you truly want your business to soar to great heights.

Consumer Surveys

There are some things that you simply can't learn from Google or Amazon. There are a number of ways to interact with your consumers, including social media and email lists, but as a beginner, perhaps the easiest way to look for a demographic that you aren't already connected with is to run consumer surveys. This can be done for many things:

- Logos and graphic art, to determine the best design from a selection of mockups, which can help improve your appearance in front of the demographic that you actually care about. For all new graphics, I like to run a short survey of at least 100 people.

- Product descriptions. Once in a while, I approach a product description in two very different ways and run a few surveys to see how people respond to them. First, I ask people to choose between the two descriptions. For the second survey, I only show the first description and ask a handful of questions about how inclined people would be to buy the product. For the last, I do the same for the other description. I compare this data to help myself determine the best approach to sell an item I plan on spending money to market.

- Demographic questions. If you have a niche but don't understand the demographics very well, using surveys to determine the age range, gender (if it applies), locations, and preferences of your demographics is a great way to begin understanding exactly who you should be marketing to and how you might want to go about it. You can also learn about the types of problems that your demographic have to begin solving these for them with your product selection. I often start with this type of survey first, and I sometimes go back and do some more demographic research to try to hone in my marketing efforts, so I'm not wasting any time or money.

- Practically anything. Seriously - if it can be formed into a question - you can ask consumers about it. Running surveys can be relatively cheap if you're willing to wait a long time for responses, so it's a good idea to run things by giant panels of people when you're uncertain about anything at all.

Now that you know how surveys may come in handy for your market research, let's discuss the method involved in running surveys.

For surveys, I generally suggest using Google Forms to create the survey itself, as this platform provides very detailed rundowns of the survey responses, especially when they are multiple choice or similar selections. Google Forms may not be completely user-friendly at first, but if you take the time to read the documentation regarding using it, you shouldn't have too many problems learning a few of the tips needed to get the best results.

Generally, a good place to find respondents is a website like Amazon's Mechanical Turk or MTurk.com. This is a micro-jobs website that allows you to pay for surveys per response or conduct small tasks that cannot be automated by computers very well but also aren't a very productive use of your time. You may also want to use this site for other means. You can find plenty of tutorials on YouTube to help you learn how to run a survey using this platform.

If any of this seems a bit too much, you always have the option of paying freelancers or survey services to help you run surveys. If you're on a tight budget, websites like Fiverr.com have providers that can respond to a very low rate. These may not be the BEST responses, but they will cost you next to nothing. Most of these providers most likely use MTurk, so you're paying a little extra just to have someone else handle the work for you.

Social Media and Email Lists

Of course, once you have put together your platform through social media websites, your blog, an email list, and any other ways of connecting with your customers, you can always directly ask your customers for their input. This can also be an excuse to promote a new product to them, but just make sure not to be too pushy and somehow reward them for any input that they give.

Communicating directly with past customers can serve to remind them that you exist, and it can also help them learn that you now have more to offer. Another great thing is that you are sure that these people are part of your demographic as you've actually successfully sold to them in the past. It's important to make an effort to build a customer base that you can later contact. This can only be done if you're building a platform in the form of a website, blog, email list, and social media, which all takes a lot of time away from trying to find products and getting them out into the market. However, if executed with regularity and care, these steps will eventually lead to profits, and you'll find that you can make more sales in less time as you launch new products in your drop shipping store.

Look at the Competition

This may be one of the most important steps for anyone trying to open and promote their own online stores. In a niche approach to selling, you will gain a lot of information by taking a look at your competition. There are two great reasons to do this. First, look at what seems to be working for your competition and understand how you can offer an equally good service, products, and overall customer experience. Next, think about how you can improve on their model. In some niches, you may be surprised to find that the top competitor isn't really doing things all that well, and that means you have a golden opportunity to seize the market by improving on their shortcomings. You will either creep up and take over, or it will begin a stronger competition that pushes both businesses to do their absolute best. Both scenarios are good for you.

When we look at our competition, there are some obvious things that we can see. Take a look at this list of questions and try your best to answer this about each online store you consider your competition.

- What products do they offer that you should offer too?

- What are their best selling products?

- What are their prices like?

- Can you match their prices?

- Can you beat their prices? A word of warning: sometimes, selling for lower than the best online price is going to cause all prices to eventually drop, making it harder for anyone to make money on it. This is especially true for those selling on Amazon, but it applies to the general market as well. However, if the lowest price is on Amazon or eBay, but your main competitor outside of those fields is selling for a significantly higher price, then it may be possible to undercut them a bit.

- Is their website well designed and easy to use?

- Do they accept most forms of payment?

- Are they truly focused on this particular niche?

- What is the quality of their website content?

These questions and anything else you may learn about your competitor help to set up a meter by which you can judge your own efforts. You can also use this type of market research to help in the niche selection process. If your goal is to find a niche that will be easy to excel in, you need to see if someone else has already done a great job in that niche first. That shouldn't stop you from going with a niche, but it does help you narrow down your final list.

In the end, failing to understand your competition is a huge mistake. While you shouldn't spend all your time trying to one-up them, you do need to make sure that you are actually a competitor yourself. To do this, you need to sneak up on them through smart strategy by creating excellent content, and providing great products with a great product description, available at fair prices.

If you're unsure of your direct competition, start looking at keywords again. Use the high competition keywords and low competition keywords, and see how often a specific website shows up in the first few pages of the search results. If a website seems to show up for all of the keywords you are considering, they may be offering all the products you intend to offer, or they may have taken the time to create content that is search engine friendly.

Return to Market Research

While we haven't discussed product research yet, it is important to understand that this is the next major part of market research. These other factors are also important, and as you begin any product research, also taking the time to handle new market research is key to truly understanding how well a product is going to be received by your demographic, how much profit you can make, and if there are new competitors that are threatening your position in a specific niche. Always taking the time to do the research and trying to understand what is happening behind those sales figures and website visitors is key to staying one step ahead and remaining relevant for years to come. Never underestimate the effectiveness of great market research.

Chapter 5
Finding the Right Product

The biggest hurdle you to overcome is choosing the right niche and the right products to focus your attention on. This decision is crucial to whether your drop shipping business succeeds or fails. The single biggest mistake you can make is choosing a product that is based on your own passions or personal interests, especially if you want to build up a truly successful drop shipping business. You have to supply what other people want, not what you want, especially if you aren't the type of person to follow trends or who is often considered to be "outside the box." I can't tell you what product to sell, but I can give you some ideas on how to choose the right ones.

How to Choose the Right Product

Without a solid product line, your business is going to face an uphill battle to become successful. With literally millions of products out there, it can be difficult to figure out what you are going to sell. The product you choose can also create other problems you will need to work through. For example, if you are planning on selling refrigerators, shipping could become a problem. If you are selling beer, there may be legal restrictions, depending on where your customers live.

Market research can seem overwhelming, but it is essential in ensuring that your product is going to appeal to the people you are going to be reaching with your site. If you have an idea of what you want to sell, you can check market trends to see how that product is currently doing on the market. If you aren't sure what you want to sell, market trends can still be useful as they can give you an idea of what products people are currently buying or are interested in buying.

Look for products that solve a problem for your target audience. If your audience is fed up with the current product offerings, find a new and better product to offer them. It can also be a great idea to choose a product that isn't easily locally obtainable or a local product that is being sold where it isn't currently available. Another suggestion is to find a product based on the interests of your target audience. This can be in the form of a new TV show or fashion trend.

This also applies to looking for an opportunity gap. If you choose a product that is already being sold by many different competitors, find something you can do better or different than everyone else. This can be an improved product feature, a market completely missed by your competitors or even something in your marketing strategy.

If you are going to sell a product based on something that is currently trending, make sure that you are capitalizing on the trend early. At the beginning of a trend, more people purchase the product. If you jump on the bandwagon at the end of the trend, everyone else is already moving on to the next thing. Unless you think you are going to revive a dying trend, don't wait too long to capitalize on a trend in the market.

When you are making your choices, it is important to consider product turnover. When dealing with a product line that changes every year, it is going to require a lot more time and energy to ensure that your product list is kept up-to-date and doesn't contain last year's products which may no longer be available. A product with a lower turnover will allow you to invest in a more informative website that is going to be applicable for a longer period.

Don't be afraid to look at smaller product categories and niches. While there may be fewer potential customers, there is also going to be less competition, and this will make it easier for you to get to the top of search engines, and it can be much more cost effective in terms of advertising. The right product is an instrumental component to your success, so take your time and don't rush into the first product that looks good.

To build up a successful business, you must be able to do one of the following:

Have access to exclusive distribution or pricing

Being able to arrange exclusive agreements for products or exclusive pricing will give you an edge on selling online without needing to buy or create your own product. These are not easy things to arrange, and you may find that you are still out-priced because other drop shippers will still sell the same or similar products at wholesale prices.

If you can get exclusive distribution rights, you need to find a way to convince your customers that the product you are selling is of better quality than the competition, especially if the competition is offering a knock-off product at a lower price. This is where the "about us" page on your website becomes even more beneficial, as it is a good place to share the fact that you have exclusivity to the product.

Sell at the lowest possible price

If you can offer your products at the lowest prices, you can steal customers from quite a big chunk of your niche market. The biggest problem is that you are doomed to fail because you simply won't be able to make a profit this way.

Low price is not always the main driving force behind a customer's decision to buy. Customers tend to want to spend their money on a product with the highest value and lowest risk. This means that you need to convince them that spending a little more money on your product is the better choice because it offers less risk and more value.

Add your value outside of the price

Think in terms of providing information that complements your chosen products. A true entrepreneur will solve problems and sell products at premium prices at the same time. Make sure you offer guidance and knowledgeable advice within your specific niche. A highly effective way to add value to your products is through your customer service. If you can answer all your customer's questions without them having to contact you, and can quickly respond to any emails, it is going to make your web store stand out.

Adding value

This isn't always easy, and this will work better for some niches than for others. Look for key characteristics that will make it easy to add value with content, especially in niches that:

Have several components

If a product is made up of several different components, potential customers are more likely to look for information on the Internet. For example, if you buy a new office chair, it's a simple purchase. If, on the other hand, you were to buy a complete home surveillance security system, you would want to know how each part of the system worked.

The more components and variety can be offered in these components, the better the opportunity to build up your value by offering information and education on the products.

If the product you are offering falls into this category, and it is not a product line that changes every year, you have a great opportunity to build up an informative site that will let your customers understand why they should buy from you. It will also help them build trust in you since you will be providing answers to all of their questions without them having to spend their time talking to someone over the phone or going into a store to speak to someone.

Are confusing or customizable

This is similar as the above – if a product is customizable or the choice is confusing, your value comes in being able to offer guidance and education on where and how to use a specific product, as well as how to customize it.

Again, if this product is from a line that isn't constantly changing, you can easily create an informative site. If the customizations are constantly changing, it may make it more difficult to build up an information hub, but it is by no means impossible, especially if the main components of the product remain the same since information on the main component is more important than customizations.

Require installation or setup

This is one of the easiest to choose – products that need to be installed or set up technically, especially if they are not easy ones. Go back to the home security system – let's say that you were choosing one, and one website offered a system with a two-page setup document and the other offered a detailed guide that ran several pages, including troubleshooting. Which one would you buy? Offering up as much information and guidance as possible is the best way to gain customers.

How to Add Value

Adding value to your product is fairly simple and can be accomplished in several ways:

- Creating detailed buyer guides

- Creating detailed listings and product descriptions

- Creating installation guides and setup information

- Creating detailed videos showing how a particular product works

- Creating a guide or system for product compatibility

Picking the best customers

Even after you have established your target market or customer pool, it is important to know that there are many different demographic types within it. You want to be aware of what demographic is going to be most interested in your product and how to best appeal to the demographic you want to target.

You can't lump all customers under the same umbrella – you might find that a customer who buys a small, lower priced item will expect you to go to the moon and back for them while a customer who purchases something more expensive will probably ask for nothing more from you than the item they are purchasing.

It is important that you target the correct demographic for your products, and the following three types of customers tend to be the best ones to deal with:

- Hobbyists

Many people have hobbies that they absolutely love, and some will spend a lot of money on equipment, tools, and training for that particular hobby. For example, some serious cyclists own bicycles that cost more than a small car, while a keen fisherman might spend a mind-boggling amount of money on equipment. Targeting the right hobbyist niche and being able to serve them with what they want will give you a real leg-up.

- Businesses

Generally, business customers are a little more price-sensitive than your average Joe, but they will order in much larger quantities. Establishing a good rapport and relationship with these businesses and earning their trust will allow you to build up a long-term business that sells in much higher volumes than by selling to individual customers. Your best bet is to pick a product that will appeal both to businesses and to individuals.

- Repeat Buyers

If you can get customers who buy from you repeatedly, it's a great business because you will have a recurring stream of income. Selling disposable products or products that need to be re-ordered frequently allows you to rapidly grow your business and build up something that all businesses need – a loyal customer base that comes back to you time and time again.

All these types of customers can be good to have, and none is really better than the other. The main reason why it is important to know where your customer fits in is so that you can respond to their needs in the most effective way possible.

Other considerations

When you are choosing a product to sell, you must take a few other considerations into account:

• Price

You must consider your price point in relation to the pre-sales service you provide to your customers. Most people will happily place an order online for $200 without needing to talk to anybody on the phone; however, if you are selling an item that costs $1,000, your customers might not be so eager. Most will want to talk to someone about the product first, and not just to get information about the item, but also to make sure they are dealing with a genuine store.

If you are planning on selling a high-priced product, you need to make sure that you can offer good phone support, and that means you and your staff need to be knowledgeable on the product that you are selling. You also need to make sure that your profit margin is sufficient to justify that level of support. Most often, the sweet spot for product prices falls between $50 and $200.

• MAP Pricing

Some manufacturers set a MAP (minimum advertised price) for their particular products, and they will require all sellers to sell at or above a certain level. This stops price wars, which is a common problem with drop shipping, and it also means that you can realize a good profit margin.

Look for manufacturers that enforce MAP pricing, and your business will gain profits immensely. With all competitors selling at the same price, it will come down to how strong and convincing your website and the sales pitch is, and you won't need to worry about being knocked out of the market by cheaper prices.

- Marketing Potential

The marketing potential of your business is the entire size of the market for your product. You want to make sure you are going to be able to get the word out about your web store to as many people within the market as possible and, to do this, you need to have an effective plan. A good plan will include advertising, often through free platforms.

It is too late to start thinking about marketing the day you launch your new business – this has to be thought about well in advance. Promoting your website is the only way you will bring in new customers, so set up social media pages, write articles, start a blog, and get involved in forums related to your niche.

- Plenty of Accessories

You can add accessories to your product to make it more versatile, useful, or attractive. They can also be used to personalize a common product and make it more individual. If the product you choose to sell has the option to add accessories, it is a good idea to include as many of them as possible in your web store, as customers like to be able to make their products their own and express their individuality.

As a general retail rule of thumb, the margins on high-priced items are lower than those on the lower-priced accessories that go with it.

Take the humble smartphone for example; most people will shop around for the best price, but when it comes to the case that goes along with it, they are less likely to do that. Instead, they will usually buy it from the same place they buy their phone from. Being able to offer compatible accessories for big-ticket items will have customers flocking in. This is especially true when you can find accessories that most other retailers aren't offering. This is a situation where using more than one supplier for your web store can prove to be exceptionally beneficial.

- Low Turnover

If you can provide information, guides, and education with your products, you are more likely to make a sale. Yet, if your chosen product is the type that changes every year, like a smartphone, it's going to be a lot of work to keep your site maintained. Stick to products that don't get updated regularly and keep your website going for much longer.

- Hard to Find

Don't be too specific here – if you sell a product that can't be found too easily locally, you stand a better chance of reaping the rewards. If a person wanted to buy a new hoe or garden fork, they would just go down to the nearest hardware store. However, selling something a bit more specific, like falcon training equipment, for example, will bring in more customers.

- Small Is the New Large

Most people expect free shipping these days, but if you sell large, expensive items, you will either lose money in shipping or you will lose customers because they won't pay the shipping fee. Keeping your products small will make it easier for you to ship out for free or very cheap.

Picking the right niche is not easy, and you first need to take a lot of different things into consideration. These are the main guidelines that you need to think about when you pick your product.

When you are in the process of choosing the product you want to sell in your web store, the options are endless, and it can be overwhelming to begin narrowing down the different products to find the one that is going to give you optimal sales and profit. By putting some thought and research into the product you want to sell, you are going to ensure that your product appeals to the customers in the target market you are striving to reach. Knowing the potential competition of a product will tell you if there is room in the market for you and how you can squeeze yourself in effectively.

Finding a valuable product will take some time and work. It will also take some work to find the accessories and add-ons that will best complement it. However, once you find these things, you are going to be able to put together an interesting e-commerce site and begin to turn a profit.

After you have found your spot in the market and made a final decision on your product, the next thing you are going to have to do is find a supplier that you can rely on to have the product you need in stock and ship it out to your customers in a timely manner.

Chapter 6
Finding The Right Suppliers

Now that you have your niche and your products figured out, it's time to find a supplier and get down to business. Finding good suppliers is very important as it may make or break your business. You don't want your business to have the reputation of being low quality. This may not be the most fun part of this business, but it is important to give every part of the business the attention and effort it deserves.

Suppliers are the ones that fulfill the order, and in a way, they are the people who represent your business and your brand. It is important for the process to run smoothly because if the supplier messes something up, your business takes the hit. An unprofessional supplier can cost you money in the long run.

When evaluating your suppliers, you first want to ensure that their English is good because good communication is key to building a relationship. If you have a good relationship, they may be able to tell you what is popular at the moment. Also, the suppliers are bound to have some connections that they may be able to hook you up with as a result of successfully building a relationship. Down the line, they may also give you a discount when they see that you can actually sell stuff through them. When you do hit it big with a product, you want to have a supplier on standby in order to ship fast.

When evaluating a supplier, find out if they have capable and experienced sales representatives who will be able to answer most of your questions in a timely manner. You also want to know the fee that the suppliers will be charging for their work, and then factor that fee into your business and see if you can still make a good profit. You want to find out early on if your suppliers do bulk orders, which will be important in later advanced stages of drop shipping since taking care of each order one by one is not a good use of time. This is definitely a good problem to have, and it is something you have to worry about only when the orders start reaching the hundreds.

Luckily, there are several marketplaces where you can compare prices and shipping times and all the different criteria in order to find the best deal. Go on Google, type your product into the search bar and look at the results. This approach is only the beginning since you won't really be able to assess the quality of suppliers and compare between them. Most drop shippers don't have great marketing and SEO and are unlikely to be easily found. Also, not every supplier will be willing to do business with you right from the start.

Dhgate.com is a website with millions of products, where you can find suppliers. This website has policies in place and their customer service department will help you if anything goes wrong with the transaction.

If you want to minimize risk, check out the suppliers under selected supplier tabs as these suppliers have deposited a certain amount, some of which you will receive in case something goes wrong. You can also check out reviews for certain suppliers on Dhgate as this will make your choice easier. Pretty much everyone will look at reviews before contacting suppliers, so they are therefore extremely important.

Reviews are pretty much the history of suppliers doing their job well, and they serve as social proof.

You can also see details like shipping time and cost which will allow you to evaluate between different choices. These days, the speed of delivery is more important than the price. If you ever need to get new products fast, you can see what is available in the 2-5 day shipping tab. This may be useful if your products turn out to sell better than you thought they would.

You can also use filters that will really help you narrow down your search based on prices, reviews, shipping time, and all the other criteria. Price is a very important criterium, but that doesn't mean you should automatically start searching for the lowest price, because, at the end of the day, it is all about quality. Quality products will ensure that you receive good reviews, word of mouth referrals, fewer returns, and happier and more loyal customers. Cheaper products can actually be quite expensive as they can cost you money in the long run. When it comes to prices, you should check out the shipping price and factor that into your final decision. Shipping time is very important as well, as dropshipping is extremely competitive. To measure how fast shipping really is, you can place several test orders.

When searching for suppliers on AliExpress, the first step is to type your product into the search bar and see what shows up. When you click on a product, you get information about the vendor. You can see how long they have been operating; the longer the supplier has been in business, the better choice it is. Working with brand new suppliers is a big risk since you don't know what can go wrong. If for some reason that information is not available, check out the supplier's products and the number of orders they've had to assess how long they have been in business for. To assess easier, sort the search results by orders.

An increasing amount of suppliers are catching onto the drop shipping trend, and some of them will outright offer to drop ship in the title of the product, so if you can find a product that meets your criteria and that also has drop shipping in the title, you already made your job a lot easier. You can also type the name of your product into the search bar and add drop shipping in the end.

If you are targeting a certain niche, the supplier may have some additional products you could sell, so keep an eye out for that. You want to keep an eye out for suppliers who have a badge of some kind as this shows that they are professional. On Aliexpress, this badge is called Top Brand Badge. You can click on this badge to find out how this badge was generated. Several criteria have to be met in order to achieve this badge, so having it is definitely a sign of quality.

If you've found a supplier you like, you can contact them by clicking the Contact now link. The best way to get in touch with suppliers is to first write them an email, and you can find good templates online that will increase the chances of the supplier replying to your email. When you talk to a supplier, you want to have questions ready because you want to sound professional. Prepare some questions about the return policy, possible additional fees, warranties, and possible price changes if you want to get a better deal since suppliers prefer people who will be working with them for the long-term.

It is better to communicate with suppliers via Skype or another platform outside AliExpress as there will be fewer restrictions. Don't be afraid to call the supplier as you need to remember that they want business and will definitely be willing to listen to new business opportunity.

Alibaba is another website by the same company where you can order items in large quantities, or in bulk. On Alibaba, you can order items directly from manufacturers for wholesale price, but you can only order in large quantities. You won't be able to order anything less than 100 items on Alibaba since it is meant for businesses.

On AliExpress, on the other hand, you can buy smaller quantities for your own consumption. I recommend AliExpress for most dropship models since with Alibaba, you are stocking items, private labeling them and then sending them to buyers yourself, which isn't really a drop shipping model anymore. Beginners should first use AliExpress and stick to it because if someone is not able to make it happen with this platform, chances are they won't be able to do it with other websites. The advantage of Alibaba is the fact that you can find the lowest prices for products, and they get lower and lower the more you order in order to utilize the economies of scale.

Also, you can find products to sell on Oberlo. Finding suppliers from all over the world and adding them to your own store can be simply done only with a couple of clicks. You find a product on Oberlo which you want to sell, import it into your Shopify store, and then the product is being sold from there. Oberlo are not suppliers, they are the middlemen, and they process the order while the actual supplier is the one who delivers the product. You should remember that by doing this, you may not necessarily be able to choose the supplier yourself, so you may end up selling subpar products. Also, this way, the delivery times may be longer than advertised. There also is no opportunity to sell branded products and to capitalize on the demand for the brand, if that is what you are interested in.

To make your drop shipping journey easier, install the Oberlo Chrome Extension for free. This extension will allow you to transport a certain product directly into your Shopify store. This extension also allows you to add additional filters when searching for a product such as shipping method, country, and currency. Based on the filters that you choose, the choices on various platforms such as Aliexpress will be highlighted in green so that you can find what you are looking for faster.

Finally, another way to find suppliers is to actually research if there are any suppliers of your chosen product in your domestic area. This requires more research, and you should already have your niche figured out to have a better chance for suppliers to accept your terms. This is the hardest approach, but if done successfully, it can allow you to have more control over the process. A great lesson to learn about entrepreneurship is that you get out of it what you put into it.

When you know which criteria are the most important to you, you can compare them across a couple of different platforms for the product you are interested in and make a choice based on that. Some products may have better quantitative data, but another platform may offer you a chance to privately label the product, which can be a game changer. There are other platforms out there to search for products in a similar way, such as SaleHoo, Doba, Wholesale Central, Worldwide Brands, Dropship Direct, National Dropshippers, Inventory Source, Megagoods, Sunrise Wholesale, and Dropified.

Chapter 7
Setting Up Your Drop Shipping Business

By now, I am sure that you have a clear understanding of drop shipping and how drop shipping orders are fulfilled. You have also selected a suitable niche, decided which products to carry in your store and identified the suppliers you are going to work with. Now, its time to move on to actually setting up your drop shipping business. However, before I take you through the process of building your business, there are a few things you need to know.

One of the things I have observed with first-time online entrepreneurs is that most of them make the mistake of assuming that building an online business is an easy process. When it comes to building a successful business, you have to adopt a long-term view and have a high level of commitment—regardless of whether it's a brick-and-mortar store or an online business. Because of the thousands of fascinating online business success stories on the internet, most people start an online business with very unrealistic expectations. If you aim to throw up a website, sit back, and expect to get a six-figure income in two months, you are going to be very disappointed. However, if you start with realistic expectations and a clear understanding of the amount of investment it will take to get you there, you will be less likely to quit when things get tough.

During the early stages of building your drop shipping business, you will have to make a major investment, either in time or money.

Investing Your Time

If it is your first time building a drop shipping business, I advise you to invest more time than money. Investing time in this crucial stage of your business will help you learn all the intricacies of business operations and gain a deep understanding of your customers and the market, which will help you make better decisions. On top of that, you will be less likely to waste your money on useless operations that are not critical to the success of your business.

It might be challenging to invest a lot of time in your new business, especially if you are working a 9-5 job and want to build your business on the side. However, the beauty of starting a drop shipping business is that it's easier to run on a part-time basis than running a brick-and-mortar business. All you need are a few hours a day or about 10 to 15 hours a week. During these early days, most of your efforts should be focused on marketing your business. As your business starts growing and the money starts flowing in, you can gradually transition into working on it full-time.

When investing time in your drop shipping business, the other thing you should keep in mind is that in the early days, you may need to put in a lot of effort and see no real results. However, once your store is up and running, you will need significantly less time to maintain it, and you will start making more money while doing less work.

Investing Your Money

If it is impossible for you to dedicate time to your drop shipping business, you may be able to grow your business by investing a bunch of money in it. However, I don't advise that, and I will always insist that if you can, you should always be out there doing most of the work and getting your hands dirty. Without a hands-on approach to the business, you will only end up wasting your money on useless operations that will not drive the overall success of the business. However, it's important to note that even if you decide to work full-time on your new business, you will still need some capital to launch the business and get operational.

Register Your Dropshipping Business

Remember that your business has to be legally registered with proper government agencies before you can start working with dropshipping suppliers. When it comes to registering businesses in the United States, three business structures are commonly used:

Sole proprietorship: This is the simplest structure you can register your business under. It has minimal filings, and your business earnings can simply be reported on your personal taxes. However, this structure offers no liability protection, which means that if your business is sued, your personal assets will also be at risk.

Limited Liability Company (LLC): This structure establishes your business as a separate legal entity, thereby providing more protection for personal assets. While an LLC offers more protection than a sole proprietorship, the protection is not foolproof. An LLC will also come with additional filing requirements.

C Corporation: C Corporations provide the most liability protection. However, registering and incorporating a C Corporation is more expensive than the other two. C Corporations are also subject to double taxation.

As a small entrepreneur, you should probably register your business as a sole proprietorship or an LLC. Personally, I feel that an LLC is the best choice for a drop shipping business. However, I would recommend that you consult with a lawyer before making a final decision on this.

After you register your business, you should then apply for an Employer Identification Number (EIN). This number is like the Social Security Number of your company. You will need to provide this number when applying for a wholesale account with your drop shipping supplier. You will also use it to file your taxes and do other official matters related to your business. You can apply for your business EIN online.

The other thing you need to do is make sure that you keep your business and personal finances separate. Blending your personal and business finances will cause confusion, make accounting a nightmare and may even get you into trouble with the IRS. The best thing is to ensure you keep the two totally separate. To do this, you should set up a separate bank account for your business, get a separate credit card, and create a separate PayPal account for your business.

Chapter 8
Pick Your Sales Channel

With the legal side of your business out of the way, you are now ready to start selling. Before you can make your first sale, you need to decide the sales channel you will use to sell your products. Where will you place your products so that prospective customers can see them? To sell your products, you have several options available. I am going to discuss the three most popular sales channels, which are eBay, Amazon, and your own online store.

Drop Shipping On eBay

eBay is the world's largest and most popular online auction site, with millions of users, and it is a good option if you want to get your drop shipped products in front of prospective buyers.

Advantages Of Dropshipping On eBay

Some of the reasons why eBay is a good option for drop shipping your products include:

Easy to set up: Selling items on eBay is very easy. All you need to do is sign up for an eBay account to start listing your products immediately. Building a store is no hassle, and there is no long verification process.

Wide reach: As I mentioned, eBay has millions of users from all around the globe. By listing your products on eBay, you get access to all these people, so your products will be visible to millions of people. Since eBay is a fairly reputable platform, people won't be afraid to buy your products off the platform either.

Less marketing: One of the biggest advantages of drop shipping your products on eBay is that you don't have to worry about the tough task of getting traffic to your products, which is one of the hardest tasks when it comes to building a business. Drop shipping on eBay allows you to take advantage of the traffic on their enormous platform.

Disadvantages Of Drop Shipping On eBay

Despite these advantages, there are some downsides to drop shipping your products on eBay. These include:

Listing fees: This is the biggest drawback of using eBay to sell your drop shipped products. Having to pay a 10% fee or higher for the successful sale of your product can significantly drive down your margins. This becomes a huge problem for drop shipping entrepreneurs since their margins are not very large to begin with.

No customization: To list your products on eBay, you will have to use the templates provided by eBay. This means that it will be a challenge to create a branded, professional, and value-added listing for your products.

Continuous monitoring and re-listing: Since eBay is basically built as an auction-style marketplace, the listings on the platform are set to expire after a certain period. This means that as a drop shipping merchant, you will need to monitor your products continuously and relist those that have expired. This can be a tedious process compared to having a static product listing. While there are some tools available to automate this process, it can still be quite hectic.

Customer relationship constraints: eBay is not built to help you build customer relationships. Sure, some customers will buy from you once or twice, but there's not much you can do to keep customers coming back to you. Your communication with customers, your branding, and your store design are severely limited on eBay, so building a loyal customer base will be a great challenge.

eBay is not an asset: If you are able to create your own drop shipping store that generates a substantial income and has a loyal customer base, this business is an actual asset that you can sell to someone else. When you drop ship your products on eBay, you won't be able to build a lasting brand or a business with a tangible value. If you decide to go out of business, you cannot sell your eBay account.

Drop Shipping On Amazon

Amazon is the number one online marketplace in the world, with yearly net sales of hundreds of billions of dollars every year. The platform attracts huge traffic that drop shipping merchants can take advantage of to sell their products. Actually, a huge percentage of the products listed on Amazon are sold by third-party merchants.

Drop shipping your products on Amazon has similar advantages to drop shipping on eBay. Getting started is fairly easy; you get instant access to millions of prospective customers, and you don't have to spend your time and money on marketing and traffic generation. On top of that, Amazon has a program known as Fulfillment by Amazon (FBA) which makes it possible for merchants to complement drop shipped products with their own products while Amazon handles the warehousing, packing, and shipping.

Despite these advantages, Amazon also has its downsides. Just like with eBay, you will have to pay commission fees in the 10% - 15% range, which take a large portion of your profits. Also, on Amazon, building long-term customer relationships is next to impossible. These online marketplaces are focused on the products rather than the sellers, so this is something you will have to deal with. You cannot customize your product listings or influence the customer experience in any way. All this is under Amazon's control. Another huge disadvantage is that Amazon has access to your sales data, which they can use to drive their own agenda. There have been cases where Amazon has been accused of using merchants' sales data to identify well-performing niches and strengthen itself in these niches, thereby pushing out the smaller merchants selling on the platform.

Selling In Your Own Online Store

As we have just discussed, drop shipping your products on Amazon or eBay is not good for the long-term well-being of your drop shipping business. If you want to avoid the disadvantages associated with drop shipping your products on online marketplaces and build a business that you have great control over, you should build your own online store. This is the method I prefer most since it allows you to be an independent entrepreneur and build your own brand. Let's see why you should build your own online store:

Advantages of Building Your Own Online Store

Full control: With your own online store, you are in control of everything—your branding, your store design, the look and layout of your product listings, etc. This allows you to decide the kind of buying experience you want your customers to have and add value for your customers, which we saw is a key element if you want to succeed in selling products online.

Better income: With your own store, you can charge higher prices because you are able to provide more value to your customers. You don't t have to pay any commission or listing fees on your own store either, which means you will earn more profits.

No competition: When you sell your products on online marketplaces like Amazon and eBay, you will have to contend with lots of competitors selling similar products, often at lower prices. Since you cannot differentiate yourself through branding, you will be reduced to competing on price, which is not healthy for any business. On the other hand, when you sell your products on your own store, there are no other sellers to compete with.

Easy design: Several platforms make it easy to build your own online store, even if you have no technical skills. There are dozens of templates available that allow you to make customizations to suit your preferences. With these platforms, your online store can be up and running in less than a day. Some of these platforms even make it possible for you to manage your business from your smartphone.

Analytics: With your own store, you have access and control over business data, including sales volumes, visitor numbers, visitor sources and demographics, and so much more. You can use this data to measure your business's performance and tweak your strategy to grow your business even further.

You build a real business: Your own e-commerce store is a real business that has its own brand. If you decide to get out of the drop shipping business, you can easily value your online store and sell it.

Disadvantages of Selling In Your Own Online Store

Traffic generation: When you sell your products on online marketplaces, you can take advantage of the millions of buyers who frequent these sites. However, when you build your own store, no one knows about it, so you will have to embark on an aggressive SEO and marketing campaign to drive traffic to your store, and this is not easy. You will have to invest a significant amount of time and money before you see substantial results. The good thing is, once business picks up, you will need much less effort to keep the business running.

Platforms for Building Your Store

Most people think that building an e-commerce store is a hard task that requires advanced skills in site building, coding, and web design. They are absolutely wrong. Anyone can build their own online store with plug-and-play platforms available online. Here, I will look at two popular platforms that you can use to build your online store. However, before I get into this, you need to know that your online store will always be a work-in-progress. If you decide to wait until you have a perfect website before you launch your store, you might never launch. Do what you can and keep improving as you move on.

While there are several platforms to build online stores, the two most popular ones are Shopify and WooCommerce.

Shopify: This is simply the best platform when it comes to building a standalone online store. Shopify takes care of all the technical aspects of setting up your e-commerce website and running it, from handling the web-hosting bits to making your site secure and processing credit card payments. By taking care of the technical aspects of your drop shipping business, they allow you to concentrate on marketing and driving traffic to your website. On top of that, they have thousands of apps that you can use to add more functionalities to your online store.

WooCommerce: This is another powerful toolkit that you can use to build your online store. WooCommerce is an open source platform that allows you to make whatever modifications and customizations you want on your site. Unlike Shopify, it doesn't have any control over your site's data, which is a big plus. However, WooCommerce is more suitable for small businesses, as managing a big store with this platform can be a bit challenging. Unlike Shopify, WooCommerce is free, but you will need to pay for licenses and buy third-party plugins in order to add more functions to your store.

Chapter 9
Marketing

Once your drop shipping store goes live and it is ready to be presented to its first customers, now is the time to get it in front of as many prospective customers as you can and attract them to become paying customers. This is one of the most challenging parts of starting a drop shipping business. However, without promoting your business, your chances of success are next to zero. Luckily, if you commit yourself and do it right, you will get massive results.

You can use several channels to promote your drop shipping business. While each business has a different channel that works best for it, I am going to look at five proven methods you can use to promote your online store. You don't have to use all of them; just focus on the methods that suit you best.

Social Media Marketing (SMM)

SMM is the use of social media sites to create brand awareness, create customer relationships, gain traffic, and drive sales. These can be done on major social media platforms such as Facebook, Twitter, Instagram, Pinterest, Google+, LinkedIn, and YouTube, as well as on online forums and blogs. While many people see social media as nothing more than a social tool, it is something that you can leverage to drive sales for your drop shipping business. When you create a social media marketing campaign for your business, you should avoid trying to market your business on every social media platform. While it might seem like a good strategy to gain maximum reach, it will be overwhelming for you, and you will end up achieving dismal results on each of these sites. What you should do is identify two to three social media platforms that will deliver maximum results and completely focus on them. All in all, social media is a great tool to market your dropshipping business, so it's a big risk to avoid using this tool.

Facebook Ads

Though it is an offshoot of social media marketing, advertising on Facebook deserves its own mention due to its effectiveness as an online marketing tool. Facebook is the largest and most popular social marketing platform in the world. The platform has over 1.71 billion monthly active users, which makes it the ideal place to advertise your drop shipping business. However, the effectiveness of Facebook as a marketing tool goes beyond the numbers. Unlike most advertising platforms that serve ads on query-based data, Facebook serves its ads based on contextual data. With query-based data, the advertising platform shows adverts that are relevant to what users are searching for on the internet. A good example of a query-based advertising platform is Google Adwords.

In contrast, platforms that serve advertisements based on contextual data allow advertisers to choose the demographics of the people they want to present the ads to. This makes it easier for you to target a specific audience. Are your products geared toward 25-year-old men living in California who have an obsession with sports bikes? With Facebook ads, you can target this exact group. Facebook advertisements allow you to choose your audience based on factors like age, geographical location, interests, behavior, job position, and so much more. This means that Facebook advertisements are more relevant and are more likely to drive conversions.

To make your Facebook advertising campaign more effective, you should first come up with a clear objective for the campaign. Is your aim to create awareness for your brand? Is it to drive people to your dropshipping store? Is it to increase your sales? Having a clear objective will help you craft an effective marketing campaign. On top of that, Facebook provides you with a variety of options that make it easier for you to achieve your marketing objectives.

To create a relevant Facebook advertisement, the other things you should keep in mind is to ensure that you use persuasive, relevant, and actionable copy, relevant and attention-grabbing images, and a clear and concise Call to Action (CTA).

Search Engine Optimization (SEO)

Search Engine Optimization is the process of fine-tuning your site to capture traffic from search engines like Google. In other words, it is the process of ensuring that your drop shipping business can be found on search engines. SEO is a broad topic that consists of many elements. However, to make it simpler to understand, SEO can be broken down into steps. The first one is defining the keywords that you want your site to rank for. This means that when people search for specific keywords, they should be able to find your site on the first page of Google. You will have to do extensive keyword research to find appropriate keywords that you want to rank for. The second step is optimizing your site for the keywords you defined in step one. Step three is building backlinks to your dropshipping store. Having many backlinks on your drop shipping store gives Google's algorithms the perception that your site is an authoritative one, which in turn leads to a higher ranking on the search engine's result page.

By properly utilizing SEO tactics, your drop shipping store will rank higher on search engines, which means that more people will find your store, visit it, and buy your products. SEO allows you to direct traffic to your dropshipping store without having to pay for it.

While performing proper SEO to ensure your store ranks high on search results is not necessarily an easy task, it is still doable. Defining the keywords you want to rank for and optimizing your store for these keywords is the easy part. The hard part is trying to outrank your competitors for the same keywords, especially when your store is still relatively new and has yet to build some authority. This is where backlinks come in handy. Backlinks from high-quality sources will help raise your store's authority.

You want to ensure that you are doing SEO correctly because according to data by Custora, organic search traffic drives about 26% of all orders on e-commerce stores. By improving your site's SEO, you can increase your sales by up to 26% percent. One thing you should keep in mind is that with SEO, you won't see immediate results. Initially, you will hardly see any results, but in the long run, you will reap exponential rewards.

Email Marketing

Email is one of the most cost-effective tools you can use to market your drop shipping business and gain customer engagement. Email generates high-quality leads and high-quality conversions, which is why it has a 44% return on investment (ROI). If you do it right, you will see massive results. Email is extremely effective because people share their contact details voluntarily, which is a sure-fire sign that they are interested in your products. Email marketing also allows you to accumulate your prospect's personal data, which you can use in further interactions. By providing quality content through email, you can create more demand for your products.

To run an effective email marketing campaign, you should have an attractive lead magnet for your site. As a drop shipping business, your lead magnet can be a loyalty program that provides subscribers with exclusive discounts. You should have a well-designed email template and ensure that you regularly communicate with your subscribers. However, this does not mean constantly spamming them with sales emails, as this will only lead to people opting out of your email list. Instead, you should always strive to provide value through your email newsletters.

Video Marketing

The greatest thing about video marketing is that it makes it possible for you to create an instant connection with your audience. Posts with videos lead to more time spent on your site and increased engagement. Search engine algorithms also tend to give more importance to videos, which means that using videos will improve your ranking, increase your conversions, and have greater results on your brand awareness campaign.

The most effective way of using videos to promote your drop shipping business is to create video reviews of the products you sell in your store. These can range from amateur reviews by previous customers to professional and detailed reviews of a product's features, performance, and benefits. If you decide on using video marketing to promote your store, create a YouTube channel that matches your store design, provide information about your business on the channel, and make sure that your channel is also optimized for search engines.

Chapter 10
Supply Chain And Fulfillment

One of the most important things to understand while using the drop shipping process is the supply chain, which is the path from the conception phase to the customers' hands. This path involves many stages, including manufacturing, shipping, and so on.

Now, a detailed supply chain of any product is often considered by some people to start all the way back to the mining of the raw materials used to make the product. However, that is a highly detailed process, and there is no need for you to know about it. What you do need to know is the supply chain related to drop shipping.

In the drop shipping supply chain, you need to know and understand what the three most important roles are, which are the following:

Manufacturers

It is the manufacturers' responsibility to create the product. In the majority of cases, manufacturers do not sell their products directly to the public. Instead, they sell in bulk quantities to retailers and wholesalers. You do have the option to purchase the products directly from the manufacturer. It will certainly be the cheapest method to buy items for resale. However, manufacturers usually have a minimum purchase requirement that you have to fulfill before you can buy the products. It also becomes your responsibility to stock and ship the products you are selling to your customers, which can be a major problem. That's why, as a drop shipper, you should go to wholesalers for your purchases.

Wholesalers

A wholesaler buys products in bulk quantities from manufacturers. The price of the goods will typically be marked up by a small margin, and the products are then sold to retailers at a new price. Some wholesalers have a minimum quantity requirement for purchases. Even so, the requirement is generally much lower than what a manufacturer will demand of you. Another important fact about wholesalers is that they buy and stock products from multiple manufacturers.

In some cases, they may even work with hundreds of them. Most wholesalers tend to operate within a particular niche or industry, like consumables or toys. Additionally, most wholesalers will not sell directly to the public and instead only sell to retailers.

Retailers

Retailers are those who sell products directly to the public. The products are almost always sold at a markup, which represents their earnings. Retailers can also use drop shipping suppliers to fulfill their orders.

Remember That Drop Shipping Is a Service

By now, you might have noticed that drop shippers do not form a part of the supply chain. If you are wondering why, the answer is rather simple. When it comes to the three roles that we spoke about above, anyone can become a drop shipper. A manufacturer might decide that it can ship the products it makes directly to your customers. In that case, it will be drop shipping the products on your behalf. Also, wholesalers and retailers can do the same. Of course, the retailers will not be offering a competitive price because it will not be purchasing directly from the manufacturer.

This is one of the reasons why you should be wary of those who claim to be offering drop shipping services. It is possible that the drop shipper is incapable of giving you wholesale pricing. An entity offering you drop shipping means that it will simply be shipping the products on your behalf. To get the best possible prices, you have to make sure that you are actually working with a wholesaler or, better yet, a manufacturer.

Chapter 11
The Complete Drop
Shipping Procedure

To actually understand drop shipping, you need to know the procedure involved. The following guide will help you further understand this.

The order process

Here is an example of how the ordering process can look like in a drop shipping process. In this example, we will take a wholesaler and an online merchant. Here, the online merchant will be drop shipping the products directly from the wholesaler.

The first step

In this step, the customer places an order with the online merchant through its online store or portal. Once the order gets approved, the following things occur.

The online merchant and the customer will receive an email confirmation of the order that has been automatically generated by the software used by the online store. Typically, both will receive identical copies of the email confirmation. The payment made by the customer will be captured during the checkout process. Then, the payment will automatically be deposited into the bank account of the online merchant.

The second step

In this step, the online merchant will place the order with the wholesaler.

The online merchant will forward the email confirmation of the order to the wholesaler. Now, the wholesaler will have the credit card of the online merchant on file, and it will be billed for the wholesale price of the item ordered. If there are any processing or shipping fees, they will also be charged together with the wholesale price.

It is possible that the drop shipper uses another method to place the order. For example, they may use automatic XML to manually place the order online. Nonetheless, emails are the most widely used method due to how easy the process is.

The third step

The wholesaler will ship the order in this step.

For the order to reach this step, the product must be in stock. In addition, the wholesaler should have been able to bill the credit card of the online merchant successfully. If these two conditions have been met, the wholesaler will pack the order and ship it to the customer directly. Now, the shipment is sent by the wholesaler. However, the name and address of the online merchant and its address will be written on the return address label. The logo and name of the online merchant will also appear on the packing slip and the invoice. As soon as the shipment is finalized, the wholesaler will send a bill along with a tracking number to the online merchant.

You might be worried about the turnaround time, but it is actually rather fast. The majority of good wholesalers will be able to take orders and ship in just a few hours. As a result, online merchants can advertise same-day shipping, even if they are using the help of a drop ship supplier with the deliveries.

The fourth step

In this step, the online merchant alerts the customer about the shipment.

The online merchant has to receive the tracking number of the order before sending the tracking information to the client. Generally, an email interface will be used for monitoring. This interface is built into the software used by the online store. Now that the order has been shipped, the payment has been collected, and the customer has been notified, the order fulfillment process is complete.

The earnings of the online merchant will be the difference between the amount that was charged to the customer and what was paid to the wholesaler.

The Customer Does Not Know the Drop Shipper

As you can see, the drop shipper is vital to the order and fulfillment process. Even so, they remain invisible to the customer at all times. Once the package is received, the client is going to find the logo and the return address of the online merchant. Nowhere does it mention the name of the wholesaler, who is the drop shipper in this case. If there are problems with the order or package, the customer will contact the online merchant, who will be responsible for coordinating with the wholesaler behind the scenes to solve issues and provide the customer with the correct order.

Drop Shipping

The responsibility of the drop shipper is to stock the products and ship them out. It has no relationship with the client. All other things related to selling such as marketing, customer service, and so on will be the merchant's responsibility.

Chapter 12
How to Compete with
Other Drop Shipping Companies

When you start your own drop shipping company, one of the problems that you are going to face is having to compete with many other drop shipping companies that may be located in the same area. If you have too much competition in your area, it will be harder for you to be noticed, especially if your competitors have already established their reputation and are well known.

You can always opt to rely on free traffic. You would rely on how well your website has been created so that people can visit your site whenever they try to search for a product that is related to your store. However, this can still be complicated. In order to stand out, you need to generate a good amount of traffic, and you can do this by using paid advertising.

You have to rely on your website to be noticed heavily and for people to come back and check the items that you are offering. First, let's focus on your website's content. Here are some of the things that you can add:

- Consider the number of linking domains - The more links you have on your website, the better your website's ranking is going to be. Remember that search engine sites will not consider duplicate links, so they will not be effective at all.

- Consider the quality of your website. It does not mean that just because you have a lot of links that your website will rank high in search engine sites. The quality of your content and how relevant the content will be will make a huge difference. You can compare the current quality of your website with others with the use of different applications. Also, when you have the right tools, you can easily check your page rank.

It is evident that if you are one of the first few websites that appear in search engine sites, you will be seen by more people. In case you do not understand page ranking, here is a guide that will let you understand the differences in each:

Page Rank 1 - 2: You have a small amount of authority. This means that you are able to reach a small amount of your target market.

Page Rank 3- 4: This is the common page rank of websites that are competing well with other websites. If you get this page rank, this means that you have a high sense of authority, and you will be displayed in one of the first few pages of search engine sites.

Page Rank 4- 5: Some websites do not get to this point anymore, because the website needs to be connected to other websites that are also considered to have high page ranks. To reach this rank, you need your website to be linked to different websites.

Page Rank 6+: It will be hard to compete in this type of page rank. You will need to employ a full-time SEO expert that will allow your website to keep up with changing times. At the same time, you need to make sure that your marketing is always in full gear. If you do not have professionals working for you, you will be lost with this type of page rank.

Deciphering Your Page Results

Do you realize that the page results that you get are different from other people in different countries who are searching for the same things that you are? This is because search engine sites consider your geographic location. This makes searching for the right items to sell easier because you are looking at what other people in the same location are interested in.

Aside from your current location, search engine sites also consider your browsing history. Again, this can alter your results from another person in the same location that is searching for the same keywords. If you want to truly see the page results without other factors altering the results, there are a few things that you can do:

1. Aside from your usual keyword, you can add a location that will make the results more specific. This is very easy to do and can already give you the result that you want.

2. Try searching in incognito mode. This will give you an unbiased ranking of the website. It will not be based on how many times you have checked that website in the past. You will see if the keywords that you have typed in are truly relevant or not.

How to Let Customers Stay on Your Website

Even if you were able to configure your website to appear first when people searched, the ranking would not guarantee that they would continue to navigate your website and actually purchase from you. To make customers stay, you need to work on your website appropriately.

- Make sure that your website has an appealing design - It helps if the design of your website is something that people find appealing. If they think that your website looks dirty with links all over the place, it will not be very pleasing to the eye.

- The design that you are going to pick out should be connected to drop shipping – You do not necessarily have to have the word drop shipping all over the website; however, your website should look like a drop shipping site with a twist.

- The navigation should be easy - If people do not understand how to get from one page to another, you can already expect that navigation will not be very easy and you will lose potential customers in the process.

- Get rid of ads that cover the whole page - One of the things that turn off a lot of people into visiting various websites is the use of advertisements. If this is something that you never liked on other websites before, why should you do it on yours?

- Allow customers to browse through your website before giving them an option to register so that they can start purchasing from your website. Remember that when you force people to register for your website, you should expect them not to want to go through with it.

- Add videos and images - Do not underestimate the power

of videos and images on your website. Each item that you sell should have images because you want people to see how the items look like. Just be specific if you think that the item may not look exactly the same as in pictures. To some, videos can be endearing, and it will make them stay on the page longer.

- Let them find what they need - You may want to put a lot of fluff, but this would be similar to having a useless PowerPoint presentation with a lot of animation. You do not need to let your website become animated to be noticed. People are on your website in the first place in order to look at your items. Let them see what items you are selling. This will make a huge difference in how long they will stay.

- Ensure your site is not laggy - Do you know one of the main reasons why people decide to navigate away from a website? It is because the website is not responding properly to the actions that they want. For example, it may take ages for an image to load. When your website is laggy, people will search elsewhere.

- If you have links, make sure that they are easy to find – Make the links that they can click on in order to get to another portion of your website visible.

- Dedicate a page on your website to frequently asked questions regarding your website, what you offer, and the things that you sell. Remember that no matter how clear you thought you had created your website, some customers will still not understand a few things. As long as you put some FAQ, your customers will know that you are trying your best to address their current issues.

Figuring Out the Rest

At this point in time, you already know how you can compete with competitors so that people start checking out your website too, but how will you know if the strategies that you are planning will actually work? The truth is, you will never know if it is going to work or not. Some people were able to implement changes to their website at the right time in order to make it easier to become established, but there are also some who may have to struggle for months before they become noticed by customers.

Chapter 13
Common Mistakes

In the drop shipping industry, many people make the same common mistakes. While these mistakes are honest and simple, they can totally wreck your business. In this chapter, we are going to explore what these common mistakes are, how they can affect your business, and how you can avoid them in your own business.

Shipping Rates

In the drop shipping business, you are going to be exposed to many different shipping rates. Vendors charge differently, and the rates can greatly differ. Many suppliers will try to compensate by charging obscene amounts for shipping, or they simply don't charge enough. It can be tough to estimate what shipping is going to cost for various orders, especially when they are being ordered from a number of different vendors. If you charge too much, you may drive customers away, and if you charge too little, you will end up eating into your profits. The best thing to do is to find the average shipping charges between the vendors you are actively using and charge flat rate shipping. You may choose to have different divisions for shipping, for example, orders under $100 may have one rate while orders over have another. This makes it easier for you to get enough money to cover shipping without eating into your profits. While some customers may end up slightly overpaying for shipping, others will underpay so it ends up evening out.

Relying on Vendors Too Much

Of course, drop shippers need to rely on their vendors as these are the people who are supplying your products for you, but there is a point where you need to be able to stop relying on them. To put it simply, you do not want to put all of your eggs in one basket.

When you rely too much on one vendor, you run into a high number of issues in your business. You might run into issues where there is an inadequate stock to fill your orders, and due to a lack of backups, you do not have any alternatives for you to fulfill order requirements. Or, you may run into an issue where the entire vendor is down for a few days or longer, and therefore your entire business is negatively affected. Relying too heavily on one vendor is not ideal. That is why when you get started with the process, you should pick at least two vendors. Over time, you will want to expand this even more. For each new product line, you should have at least two vendors who can supply your products for you. This will keep you from running out and having to issue refunds or informing paying customers that their orders will be delayed and that you will not be able to honor your promised shipping rates and times.

Expecting it to Be Too Easy

While drop shipping is a relatively simple business that can be automated to provide you with a passive income stream, it doesn't mean that you won't have to do any work to earn your income stream. If you want to grow your business, you need to be prepared to put in the work. Setting up your business is the hardest part; it will take most of your time and a lot of effort to make sure everything is in place. Once your business is completely set up, the management process becomes significantly easier.

If you have the resources, you might want to hire some help. While this may be a little preemptive, having people on board who are experienced with business launches can significantly increase your growth rates and make it easier for you to expand at your desired rate.

This business is certainly easy to get into, but it does still require you to put in the work. Do not believe that you can simply slap together a couple of things and have a totally functional six-figure business. You will need to put in the work to build your business to earn the profit you desire.

Not Enough Branding Display

When you are running a drop shipping company, your brand is not attached to products. While other companies have their brands and logos displayed all over products, your products will display other people's logos or none at all. As a result, you need to ensure that you have your brand displayed adequately in all other areas of your business. Your website, social media pages, emails and anything else that allows you to interact with the customer should have your brand on it. All of your marketing campaigns should have your brand included as well. It is important that you do your best to market your brand as effectively as possible. That way, people will remember who you are, even though their products don't have your brand name on them.

Difficult to Access Order Information

When a customer orders an item from you, they want to be able to identify where their order is and when they can expect to get it. Many drop shippers do not consider this aspect and fail to make the order information easily accessible. For enhanced customer service experience, you should make this information accessible to every single customer who purchases through you. You can do this easily by having automated emails that send out information regarding the shipment. On the email, include information such as the order number, when the order was purchased, the purchase price, what is included in the order, and when the order is expected to arrive. You should also provide easy to use instructions regarding what customers can do if they are unhappy with their order or if they experience any issues with the shipping process.

Not Enough Emphasis on the Customer

Because of how automated the drop shipping business is, it can be easy to forget how important your customer is to your business success. Many drop shipping companies fail to recognize the importance of their customers and therefore end up accidentally providing a difficult and undesirable customer experience. As a result, they may end up losing a significant number of potential leads and gaining negative feedback from customers who did go through and purchased products from the company.

Even though there are many important aspects of your business, such as your website and marketing tactics, your customer is always the most important part. If you do not focus on your customer, you will end up creating a business that does not serve their needs, and therefore, you will have a failing business. A business that does not attract clients is a business that does not earn income. Always remember that.

New business owners make many mistakes, and this is completely normal. Drop shipping companies feature a significant amount of automation, and this can, therefore, make it even easier for you to run into mistakes that you didn't initially think of. You should think of your retail store like a machine. Each part of the machine needs to operate efficiently if you are going to have a business that effectively serves your target market and earns you a six-figure income. Make sure that you recognize these mistakes and set yourself up to avoid being affected by them in your own business so that you don't face the potentially lethal side effects that they can have on your success.

The end... almost!

Reviews are not easy to come by.

As an independent author with a tiny marketing budget, I rely on readers, like you, to leave a short review on Amazon.

Even if it's just a sentence or two!

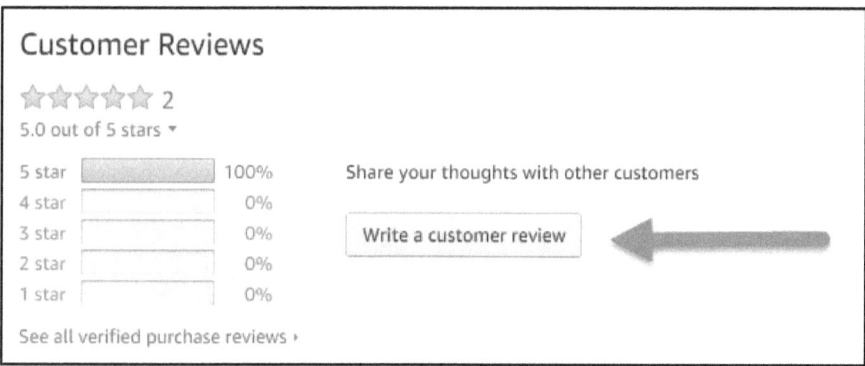

So if you enjoyed the book, please...

>> Click here to leave a brief review on Amazon.

https://www.amazon.com/review/create-review?asin=XXXXXXXXX

I am very appreciative for your review as it truly makes a difference.

Thank you from the bottom of my heart for purchasing this book and reading it to the end.

Chapter 14
Exit Strategies

Every business, even an e-commerce business, needs a solid exit strategy. There are two reasons why you may need to use your exit strategy: either you are not earning enough, or you do not want to keep the business, and therefore want to sell it. Regardless of your reason, having a strong exit strategy in place will ensure that you are prepared for when that time comes.

Exit strategies are simple to create and should be reviewed regularly. Make sure that you are well aware of the terms that surround your exit strategy so that you can be prepared for when your business hits the point where you are ready to make an exit. While it may not come for many years, maybe not even in your lifetime, if you choose to pass the business down, having an exit strategy in place and regularly reviewing it is important.

Close Down or Sell

If you are running a business that is not thriving, it may be time to deploy an exit strategy that allows you to shut down your business. While in some cases you can simply shut down shop, in others you may still need to have orders fulfilled and inform existing customers that you are closing. If you are going to close down shop, make sure that you do so effectively. You never want to leave your customers hanging because this can lead to you having a difficult time launching a new business and gaining trust in the future. Yes, just because you close down one store does not mean you can't open up a new one in the future.

If you are running a business that is successful or better yet, thriving, you may want to consider selling your business. This way, you don't take a loss or simply have the income stop flowing. Instead, you can sell your business to someone else who wants to keep it running, and you can earn a profit from the effort you put into building your business and getting it to the level that it is now. If you want to sell your business as an exit strategy, it could be because you are not interested in staying in business, because you are looking to make a change in career, because this was the plan all along, or because it has reached a point where you are no longer interested in keeping it going. Regardless of the reason, you should do your best to identify it early on and create a strategy around that plan.

Business Appraisals

Before you sell your business, you need to appraise it. Many things go into the appraisal of your business, and you may want to consider hiring a professional appraiser to help you with this process as they will be able to give you the most accurate value of your business. The appraisal is more than just knowing how much gross revenue and profit you earn from your business every year, as it also factors in the amount of potential growth that can be expected and the strength of the foundation that the business was built on.

Before you sell your business, you will always want to appraise it. This will allow you to know what is your worth. Knowing the true worth of your business means that you can negotiate more effectively and accept offers that are actually reasonable to the value of your business. If you don't know this number, you shouldn't be selling your business just yet.

The Selling Process

Selling a business can be difficult. Just because the business has a certain value, it does not mean that you are going to get that value from a potential buyer. In fact, you may initially not get any offers at all. In other cases, you may sell the business almost immediately for asking price. For your best interest, you should go into the process with the expectations that you are going to have to be patient and wait for a seller. This keeps you from having to rush and jump on any low baller offer that is tossed your way.

Many people are looking for "turn-key" businesses or businesses that they can buy and maintain as they are and simply earn profit from. They do not want to have to invest a significant amount of work into earning their profit, at least not initially. They simply want to step into the driver's seat and expand the business as rapidly as possible without having to put any work into the foundation. The more established your business already is, the more opportunity you will have to sell it to potential buyers.

You should be prepared to negotiate with your potential buyers, as they are likely to come to you with a low offer. If they do, you need to know what the value of your business is and the lowest amount that you are willing to settle for. Still, you want to negotiate to bring their number up to as close to the valuation as possible. The more valuable your business is, the more you need to negotiate as this is when more complex deals come into play.

Something that most businesses offer that you should be prepared to offer as well is a limited amount of ongoing support. You should be prepared to offer the buyer at least 30 days of support with email systems and guidance so that they can learn to take over the company seamlessly. This gives them the opportunity to have a smoother take over instead of them stepping in and not really knowing how you have run your company until this point. It also assists with the sale process as people like knowing that they will be guided to take over your success instead of putting into the seat of a car they don't know how to drive.

Remember, just because you reach the negotiation process with a certain potential buyer, it doesn't mean you are going to make a sale. You might negotiate with many potential buyers before you reach a deal that actually meets the needs of your business. Don't feel obligated to make a sale just because you have entered the negotiation phase with a potential buyer. In fact, reaching this stage and leaving it if the clauses aren't promising can work in your favor. In some cases, when a buyer is particularly motivated, threatening to reject the deal altogether can encourage them to come closer to your desired value. It shows them that you have decided what you want for the business and that you are not willing to sell for any less. It also shows that your company is actually valuable because you aren't willing to sell it off for any ballpark number.

When to Sell to?

As aforementioned, you will likely have your own reason as to why you are starting your business in the first place. If you are going into business with the intention to build a six-figure business, you likely want to keep it running until you no longer desire to run it. However, you may also want to sell it when it reaches a certain valuation so that you can walk away with a lump sum from the business.

When you decide to sell your business will largely depend on what your intention with the business is. Once you have decided what will trigger the sale, you need to pick the perfect time to get into the market and sell your business.

The first thing you need to consider is the state of your business. A company that is on an upward trend in terms of profit and traffic is one that will have greater sales potential and a higher valuation. People want a business that is growing, not one that has reached its peak or that is beginning to dwindle. When your business is thriving, it is a good time to consider entering the market for the sale of your business.

Another thing to consider is the state of the current market. While businesses will almost always sell well, a recessed market may result in you having to settle for less than your business is worth just to make the sale. If you are not willing to take a hit on your sale price, you will want to wait until the economy comes back up so that you can earn your desired value from your business.

Once your business and the market are in the right position, you can consider selling your business off. This will provide you with the opportunity to earn a large amount of capital off of it which you can invest elsewhere. With that money, you may consider starting a new business venture or investing in one that you are already operating so that you can grow it significantly. That is completely up to you.

Having a strong exit strategy in place for your business is extremely important. Any business, even one that is anticipated to stay in business for a long period of time, needs to have an exit strategy. There are many reasons as to why you may want to exit your business and having this strategy in place can give you the opportunity to make an efficient exit that will not damage your success or profits. Make sure that when you are in the process of creating your business plan, you include an effective exit strategy that will allow you to exit the market properly when you are ready. An improper exit strategy can lead to selling prematurely, losing money, or otherwise running into a rookie mistake with your exit strategy.

Chapter 15
Tips for Successful Drop Shipping

Now that we have taken some time to look into drop shipping and how to start your own business, it is time to take a look at a few tips that you can follow to get the most out of this business model. Drop shipping is a simple idea, but it does take some work to get things up and running. The following are some tips that you can follow in order to make your business as successful as possible:

Focus on Marketing

When you get started with your own drop shipping company, you have to take some time to focus on marketing. Even if you plan to list your products on eBay or Amazon, you still have to spend some time marketing your products to stand out from the crowd. Remember - there are many other sellers and drop shippers out there who are trying to compete in the same market as you. If you don't take the time to market your products and your page, you will end up getting lost in the crowd and won't make any sales.

We talked about many different ways to market your products, and as a business owner, it is important that you learn how each one can help you grow and scale your own business. You may find that SEO is the best choice for you, especially if you have your personal website to sell the products. You may find that spending some time on social media is a better option.

Drop Shipping

All of these methods can work well, but if you are able to think of a new method, one that has you go outside the box rather than just using traditional methods, then consider using it. Dropshipping is an industry that has a lot of competition, so finding ways to stand out from the crowd can make a big difference in how successful you will be.

Do Not Underprice the Products

We have talked about this one a little bit, but remember to be careful about how you price your products. Some drop shippers will try to beat the competition by lowering the prices of their products by quite a bit. They think this is a surefire way to convince customers to work with them. While this may seem like a good idea, and some customers do like to look for a good deal, it can backfire on you on occasion.

Many customers know the price of other products, or they know how to search online and compare. If they see that the price you are listing at is too low, they will be wary and assume that they are going to get a substandard product that they don't want, and you won't be able to make many sales in the process.

At the same time, you won't be able to earn as much income in the process either. The lower you make the price, the less profit you are able to make on that item. If you price it too low, the shipping and other costs will take up any profit that you make, and if you aren't careful, it is possible that you owe money instead of making any.

Pick a Product That Makes a Good Profit Margin

When starting out your new business, there are a lot of drop shipping products to choose from. However, you need to make sure that you choose products that are going to earn you a good deal of profit in the process. If you are only going to earn $1 on each product, it is probably not a good option, as you would have to sell thousands of those each month to make any profit on them at all.

The higher the profit margin on the item, the better it is going to be for your business. You can sell a good amount of items, and make a ton more money in the process. Finding products with at least a 45 percent margin after you pay for shipping and taxes can be great too. Also, if you can find products that make a profit of $100 or more, that is even better.

How do you make sure that you find products that will make you a good amount of profit? First, go through your supplier's pages and decide which products you are most interested in. Then, you can take a look at how much each of those products costs for you to purchase from the supplier. With that number in mind, go online and see how much other suppliers are charging for that same item.

The last step is important because you want to make sure that your products are priced in a competitive manner. You want to get the most out of the pricing, but you also need to be careful not to price too high compared to competitors. If you look at the price that the supplier is charging and compare it to the price others are charging for that item, and you see that the profit margin is too low, it is time to move on to a different product. Take your time and search around until you are able to find the right products that will make you enough money to make the process worth your time.

Find Ways to Bundle Items Together

As a drop shipper, it is your job to find ways to make your business stand out. One way to do this is to bundle some of the items that you are selling together. This can be beneficial both for you and your customer.

Many customers want their shopping experience to be as pleasant and swift as possible. They don't want to spend hours looking online for items that go together or will work together. If you are able to provide them with a bundle of items they need in one spot, and you can even provide it with a little discount, they are more likely to make the purchase.

This method is going to benefit you as well. When you get the customer to purchase the bundle, that means a bigger sale for you, and if you can find a way to turn it into a subscription service, where the customer will purchase the same bundle or product every month, you can keep earning the same income from it over and over again.

Pick the Platform That You Like Best

We spent some time talking about different platforms that you can use to start this kind of business. With each one, you will be faced with advantages and disadvantages, and it is up to you to choose which one seems like the best one for your needs. Some of the bigger sites, like Amazon, Shopify, and eBay can be nice because they already have a lot of name recognition, so you will already find many customers there.

However, there are also advantages that come with selling on your website. You get more choices with the templates that you want to use and have more options regarding how the website works. And, in the long run, these personal websites often end up being cheaper to use and maintain compared to other options.

Always Provide the Best Customer Service

Customer service is always important, and it is definitely something that you need to pay attention to when it comes to selling your drop shipping products. There is going to be a ton of competition out there, and one of the ways that you can make yourself stand out from the crowd is to provide the customers with the best service possible.

There are many different methods that you can choose to help you do that. You can make it easy for the customer to email or contact you and ask any questions that they may have. You can bundle your products and services together to make things easier and even cheaper for your customers. In some cases, sending along a little gift, a personalized note, or even another special offer can help to provide great customer service that they are going to appreciate and that will keep them coming back in the future.

Order the Product Yourself Before Selling it

This can be a great method to get the same experience that your customer would when ordering from you. It is also a good way to ensure that you are picking out the right supplier for your needs. If you go through the whole process just like your customers do, you will see potential issues, and you can decide if that supplier is the right one for you or if you need to pick someone else.

To do this process, simply go to the supplier page and order one or more of their products, specifically the ones that you would like to sell to the customer. Fill in all the information and choose the shipping options that you will provide to your customers. Then, sit back and wait.

When the product arrives, note how long it took and whether or not that time frame is within the amount the company had promised. Take a look at the packaging and how professional it looks. Open the box and look at the product, determining if it is the right product by checking if it is made out of high-quality materials, and more. Basically, you want to consider whether or not you would be happy with this product and its speed of delivery if you had actually purchased this item for yourself.

If you are considering working with a few different suppliers, it is best to do these steps with each one. If you want to see which company is better than the other when it comes to similar products, order at the same time from them and see what happens. You can compare shipping prices, shipping time, the price of the item, and the quality of the item when it gets to you.

If you encounter any issues with the company you want to work with, then it may be best to pick out a different supplier. Don't assume that it is just a one-time thing. You are the face of the business, and if a supplier isn't able to provide a good service and impress your customers, you are going to be the one who is blamed. If there are any problems, consider working with someone else to ensure you give the best customer experience to anyone who purchases from you.

Starting your drop shipping business can be an exciting time. You have to figure out which products you would like to sell, which supplier is best to work with and make sure that you are pricing and marketing the items so that your customers are able to find them. When you are ready to get started with this new business model, make sure to check out these tips to make it a little bit easier for you.

Conclusion

Starting a drop shipping business is an incredible way to earn yourself a six-figure income. There are many ways to start a drop shipping business, but this streamlined guide will allow you to start one efficiently and reach your six-figure income as quickly as possible. Even though drop shipping is a passive income stream, you should be prepared to put in a fair amount of work to establish your business. Once you establish your business and have regular sales on your website, you can hire assistants and remove yourself from the business, making it an even more passive income source.

I hope that this book was able to clearly guide you through the process of starting your own drop shipping business. Each chapter was designed to be a clear and concise guide walking you through each step of the business so that you can start with a strong plan. By following this guide, you will certainly be able to start your own business with the potential to earn you a six-figure income.

The next step is for you to start putting these plans into action. If you haven't been working step-by-step throughout the book, then it is time to go back to the beginning and start implementing the strategies to develop your drop shipping business. Make sure that you pay close attention to the common mistakes and tips and tricks that have been outlined in this book as they will provide you with the knowledge you need to strategize and have a strong start in your drop shipping business. That way, you can ensure that you set yourself up for total success.

Thank you, and I wish you the best of luck in creating your six-figure drop shipping business.

DOWNLOAD YOUR FREE GIFT BELOW:

These 14 New Habits Will Double Your Income, from Today

An Easy Cheat Sheet to Adopting 14 Powerful Success Habits:

Stop Procrastinating and Start Earning with Intent Now!

Are Your Bad Habits Keeping You from the Life You Want?

Mine definitely were, but then I dedicated myself to *new habits* – and everything changed!

Most people get stuck in same old routines. We eat the same breakfast, we talk to the same people. Human beings are creatures of habit, and it locks us into negative cycles we don't even know are there.

Drop Shipping

Like me, you've had enough of the same-old, same-old. It's time for change!

This guide gives you the 14 most high impact habits that helped me double my income nearly instantly, when I set out on this journey. I will help you change, and I'll make it stick!

This FREE Cheat Sheet contains:

- Daily success habits that the most successful people in the world live by

- Common, but little-known habits that will surprise you

- Details on what Stephen Covey, Oprah Winfrey, Elon Musk, Bill Gates and Albert Einstein did that you aren't doing to maximize your earning potential

- Tips on how to overcome habit fatigue

- The reality of adopting difficult, challenging habits and the rewards that result

Scroll below and click the link to claim **your cheat sheet!**

It's tough to admit that you're doing it wrong. I went through it, and it sucks. After that I was free to change however necessary, to meet my goals. I want you to know that change is waiting for you. This guide is so easy to follow, and if you put it to work in your life – you will double your income.

Adopt these habits, and change your life.

CLICK HERE!!

Check Out Our Other *AMAZING* Titles!

Book 1: Passive Income Ideas For 2020: A Step by Step Guide to Easy Passive Income Ideas For 2020 and Beyond.

Leverage Social Media

"He who makes $25,000 annually through passive income is more enviable than he who earns $100,000 annually through a salary."

— *Mokokoma Mokhonoana*

Drop Shipping

Everyone and their grandmother are on social media nowadays. The opportunities created by social media as a new kind of jobs and businesses have emerged thanks to social media. People across the globe can communicate with ease nowadays thanks to many social networks out there. There is also something for everyone depending on what you are into. If you want to connect with family and friends, Facebook might be for you. If you want to know what is happening now or trending, then you might be a Twitter person. Those that like to share their day to day lives through short videos can consider Snapchat. Instagram is for the people that value photography and beautiful aesthetics while Pinterest is what you may want your life to look like. It offers ideas on décor, fashion while still being informative. For those that want to learn how to do anything and connect with people with similar interest, consider YouTube. If you are into messaging and sharing funny memes, WhatsApp may be more up your alley. These are just a few of the popular social media sites out there, and more are coming up every day.

With Facebook having 2 billion, Instagram with 800 million and Twitter with 330 million active users every month, it is no wonder many companies have stopped ignoring social media as a place to market their products. As of 2017, many big companies and SMEs had added more money to their social media marketing budgets. Since then, more and more companies have recognized the power of influencers is selling their product on social media.

How to Find your Niche on Social Media

It's sad to say that there is nothing new that you can come up with to attract an audience on social media today. Everyone does the same things, but they add their personality to it. All you need to do is look for something that you are good at and are willing to pursue it to the end and do it better than any other person in that niche. If you want to be a makeup artist, learn the craft and do something different that people have not seen before.

Creativity on social media is what separates those who make it from those who don't. It is good to stick to one niche at a time on social media so that you can grow and become an authority on that niche. Be the person people search for when they are looking for new techniques to apply to make up for example. Be the one to put people on new products in the market. This way people trust your opinion and brands recognize your influence over your community. You can use this influence to get paid to introduce new products to your audience.

There is also such a thing as being too niche. People get bored quickly if they can predict the next content. Be unpredictable but don't stray too far from your niche. It's also good to look at what other people in your niche are doing so that you can get a clear view of where your niche is at. Look at what is popular and incorporate it but also consider what is missing and add that to your content. Research and see if your niche is scalable and leverage your audience to make yourself some money.

After picking a niche you know, you can be good at, ensure you pick the right social media platform for you to start working on. I know it is tempting to be visible on all social media platforms but it rare for someone to do a good job if they are giving less than 100% on each platform. At most, pick two of your favorite and work on those. Once you have a following, your followers you follow you wherever you are. Pick a platform that suits your niche. If it requires visuals consider YouTube, If it requires an online store, Facebook and Instagram may do the job.

Case Study: How to Make Money on Instagram

Let's look at one social media platform and see how you can make money from it. Instagram was initially as a platform to share photos with family and friends, but it has transformed to be more professional. Large and small businesses alike are using the platform to attract more customers. Some people have been able to leverage the business side of Instagram and their followers to make a good living off it.

- Leveraging higher numbers

An account with more following and a good engagement can reach out to smaller accounts in the same niche and offer to help them out at a fee. It may be mentions or a collaborative post depending on the terms agreed, but the smaller channel will get quite some followers from the larger account. This will only work if the two accounts have similar content and niches because followers will only follow what they are into. There are also niche engagement groups on Telegram and Instagram's Direct Message that charge a one-time fee to join where small accounts can interact with more influential accounts. They offer engagement boosts where people in the group can collaborate, make money and connect with each other.

- Sponsored Content

We have all seen that #ad on some of our favorite personality's posts. That means that they are collaborating with a product to introduce a product to their audience. It can either be a video, a mention or a series of posts depending on what the person and the brand agreed upon.

The person called a social media influencer gets paid a certain amount to put up that post on their account. They may be seen in an event hosted by the brand, they may take photos with the photo they are advertising, or they may do a full review of the product. Larger accounts can charge a company by the hour the post stays up on their page while some may charge per post. The influencer charges based on the social reach, potential leads and eventual customers that buy from the brand from their following. With Instagram, companies can either pay for advertisement on your feed or on Instagram stories. It is important to sign contracts with the brand you are working with so that you ensure you get paid for your work. A contract is also important because it clearly states what is required of both parties.

- Flipping Instagram Accounts

It is a familiar process where an influencer can buy a small account, grow its followership and sell it at a higher price. They don't have to do a lot because they can boost engagement from their account. It is still a slow process, but it gives better returns.

- Selling your Products

If you have the numbers and already know how to market on Instagram, the next step is selling your products to your audience. You already know what they like and have enough feedback to create a product that solves a problem. You can also open an online store and start selling to your followers which is a way many people are making money on Instagram. Since Instagram is a visual platform, many creatives have used it to market their art. Photographers and videographers are some of the people that have benefitted the most from showcasing their work on the platform. People have gotten high paying contracts to work with some of the biggest brands by tagging them on work; the creator thinks the brand may like. Apps like Stylinity allow your followers to purchase content from their favorite influencers. With every purchase that is made, you can earn a commission from soothing that is already free on your page.

- Managing Other People's Instagram Accounts

If you have been on Instagram for a while and understand its algorithm, it can be easy for you to become a social media manager. You just have to take the content which the owner of the account sends you and post it at the best time with appropriate content. Depending on your arrangement, you may also handle replying to comments and direct messages. Social media management is a freelance skill that is in high demand today especially for big companies or personalities that don't have the time to deal with social media themselves. Some companies that offer services hire social media managers to answer peoples queries online and offer solutions. You can also be a consultant and offer advice to passional brands on the best strategies to grow and connect with their audience.

- Being a Brand Ambassador

This is quite similar to sponsored posts except you are the face of the brand. You will be required to attend launches and regularly speak about the brand to your audience. You will also need to use the brand's product exclusively depending on what is agreed upon by both parties. In exchange, the influencer gets paid regularly by the company. Look for unique brands an approach them for a long-term partnership. The best way to land a brand ambassador job is if you grow your personal brand and have a target following that a brand may want to associate with.

- Affiliate Marketing

You can promote products on your page by linking their links wither in the bio space or on Instagram Stories. People are more likely to buy if you give an honest view of the products and it solves a need they have. They will also buy if it is in your page's niche.

Book 2: Mastering the Millionaire Mindset

A Secret Blueprint to Success for the World's Rich and Powerful (Millionaire Master Plan)

Factors that Drive Success

"The key for us, number one, has always been hiring very smart people."

- Bill Gates

Before we dive deeper into the book, it might be good for us to rehash what we've learned along the way so far. In the earlier parts of the book, you were briefed on the importance of developing a millionaire mindset and why that's important in becoming financially independent. Also, you were exposed to the many problems and challenges that people face with regards to their finances. We also talked about the necessary first steps that you need to take in order for you to get the ball rolling towards achieving financial freedom. Now, you need to be exposed to the many different variables and factors that might determine your success in your endeavors.

The reason that you have to be aware of these factors is that these concepts can actually help the way that you choose to structure your life. To put it simply, you are able to give your actions a better sense of purpose if you know what kind of impact they can have on your goals. For example, one of the essential factors that we will touch upon today is the development of one's intellectual capacity. If you know that getting smarter is going to lead towards success, then you can structure your daily habits around trying to fuel your knowledge and increase your intellectual capacity. Awareness of these factors and variables can only help you in setting your goals and your action plans for yourself.

In this chapter, you are going to be exposed to three important factors in particular. First, there is intellectual capacity. As an entrepreneur and thought leader, you are limited by what your mind can comprehend. So, if you have a limited intellectual capacity, then it's going to be very difficult for you to develop certain skill sets that can give you a competitive edge. Next, there is the factor of one's social skills. Obviously, there is no way for you to be able to do everything on your own. You need to be able to tap into the resources that are made available to you by the people who surround you. Lastly, we are also going to talk about the importance of maintaining integrity and reliability with the way that you work.

Intellectual Capacity

Why is it that Bill Gates finds it so important to hire smart people for his business? Is there really any truth to the idea that kids who get high grades in school are the ones who end up becoming more successful in the future? How smart do you have to be in order for you to achieve your goals? These are some of the questions that we are going to try to answer in the initial part of this chapter. Gates himself admitted that his method of hiring is rather elitist. But is that such a bad thing?

A Case for High IQ

Actually, there is some research that suggests that smarter people tend to make for better workers. Based on parameters set by *Psychology Today*, IQ encompasses various aspects of cognitive function, namely, problem-solving, language acquisition, and spatial manipulation. A standard IQ test would encompass all of these aspects. Typically, someone with a score of 100 on an IQ test would be considered average. Testers who score above 125 fall under the top 5%.

According to an article published by the *Harvard Business Review*, there are three areas of performance in which employees are evaluated: ability, social skills, and drive (Chamorro-Prezumic, Adler, & Kaiser, 2017). The authors of the article stress that when it comes to determining an employee's potential, companies have to gauge how likely it is that an individual would be able to learn or master complex skills. And the best way to gauge one's potential is through IQ or cognitive ability.

One of the most popular resource materials that make a case for hiring people with high IQ levels is a paper that was published in the *Journal of Personality and Social Psychology* back in 2004. The research was spearheaded by Frank L. Schmidt and John Hunter. In a nutshell, what their research found is that smarter people tend to perform better in the workplace because they were better and faster at learning new skills.

Increasing Your IQ

Don't worry if you don't have an IQ score that falls within the range of the elite. Like any other skill in life, your intellectual capacity is something that you can practice and build on overtime. In order for you to be truly successful, you need to invest a lot of time in yourself. This means you making a concerted effort to sharpen your mind and hone your skills. The deeper you invest in yourself, the better you will become at handling daily problems and challenges that any entrepreneur or professional might face. In order for you to really grow your intellectual capacity, try to follow these tips:

1. Work on your imagination. Remember that any kind of success only comes out of imagined results, opportunities, and possibilities. If you force yourself to be more imaginative with the way that you think, then you are essentially expanding the realms of possibility for you to succeed. With a strong imagination, it will be easier for you to solve problems, expand networks, and build strong connections with the people you work with.

2. Put yourself outside of your comfort zone. As much as you might not want to hear this, real growth and development take place outside of one's comfort zone. This is what it means to expand your horizons. If you only stick to environments and projects that you're already familiar or comfortable with, then you are stymying your own growth. You should always give

yourself a chance to gain a new perspective by immersing yourself in situations that you've never been in before.

3. Never be without a book. If you survey all of the people in the world who are generally deemed successful, it's likely that all of them have a habit of reading books. Carving a few minutes or hours out of your day to engage in reading can really help expand your worldview and sharpen your intellect. When you read, you are essentially engaging in a one-sided conversation with the author. Any book that you read, whether good or bad, is always going to reveal to you something that you never knew. If you're not a big fan of reading, audiobooks can help too.

4. Try your hand at brain teasers and tests. Pick up a sudoku or a crossword puzzle every now and then. Download apps on your phone that are designed to sharpen your cognitive function. Play memory games or speed-thinking exercises. Participate in problem-solving activities. All of these experiences help build the neuroplasticity of your brain. This means that your brain is going to get better at forming neural connections. As a result, it is able to function at higher levels. Like any other muscle in your body, if you consistently exercise your brain, it gets stronger.

5. Make learning a habit. This is a point that is going to be elaborated upon further in a later chapter. But in a nutshell, you should always consider yourself as a student. You should never stop trying to learn from other people or from reliable source materials. When you are constantly feeding your brain with new information, then you are also widening your knowledge base.

6. Exercise regularly. You might not think that running on a treadmill can make you smarter, but it really does. When you

have a solid and consistent exercise routine in place, you are essentially improving your body's ability to absorb oxygen. And your brain actually functions better when it is full of oxygen. Hence, physical exercise can also help strengthen the brain. Some of the benefits that come with having a brain that is full of oxygen include improved memory, focus, and cognitive function.

7. Practice good sleeping habits. Not getting enough sleep can dramatically impair your cognitive function. Hence, you put a limiter on yourself whenever you're just running on fumes. Getting enough rest and recovery while you sleep is essential to priming your mind for a day full of learning and cognitive activity.

Book 3: Instagram Marketing 2020:

The Playbook for Increasing Your Following and Generating Profits

Tips For Every Brand

There is no time like the present to capitalize on the boom that Instagram is experiencing. Instagram has more than one billion users, and this number is steadily increasing. Different features, as well as functions, are regularly introduced by this platform. Any hype that you heard about Instagram is real. However, the algorithm of this platform keeps changing frequently, and this can prove to be a rather tricky part for a lot of brands that are trying to maximize their engagement rate. The changes in the Instagram's reach aren't as severe as the ones on Facebook because of the latest update. In your best interest, it is undoubtedly prudent to ensure that you are indeed following the best practices suitable for Instagram. Regardless of whether you're new to Instagram or are trying to optimize your reach on this platform, the tips given in this section are certainly worth going over. So, here are specific tips, which you must keep in mind while using Instagram.

Don't Ignore The Bio

A common mistake that a lot of brands make when using Instagram as their marketing platform is that their sole focus tends to be only on the photos and captions that they use. They concentrate so much on these two aspects of Instagram that they forget about another essential part of their Instagram profile: their bio. The bio of a brand is as important as the content posted on this platform. Instagram bio is an incredibly valuable space of real estate in the virtual world. The bio can be used as a call to action button, or it can also be used for directing visitors to any promotional campaigns you're running. There is a lot that you can do by using the bio space.

Here are a few things that you must include in your bio regardless of what your brand is about.

You must have a custom hashtags that other users, as well as your brand, can use for tagging and sharing. It creates relatability and boosts visibility and engagement on Instagram. You can also use the bio for adding a relevant link to your business website or homepage to direct any traffic. You can also use the bio to hide any Instagram-specific promotional links. Did you know that you could include a URL tracker in the bio to analyze your Instagram traffic? You must include a brief description, motto, or a slogan, which conveys your brand's objective to the visitors of the page.

Start Using Instagram Stories

Essentially, this tip will help optimize your content strategy for Instagram. One of the most popular features introduced on Instagram is their Story tab. The Instagram Stories feature is quite similar to the Snapchat Stories, which were quite popular a few years ago. Instagram stories are among the most popular type of content feature being used by brands these days. This feature is time-sensitive, and its self-destructive model of content is what attracts the users to use it.

Other features, like audience polls, along with Stories' ads, have become quite common on Instagram. All these things indicate that the platform is actively encouraging brands to use Instagram in their promotional activities. If you want to increase your engagement rate, then make it a point to update your Instagram Stories regularly. The best part about using this feature to promote your brand is that there is no expectation of perfection. Your Instagram Story does not need to be polished or professionally shot. It can be a combination of a small post, selfies, snapshots or anything else. It is an excellent way for a brand to connect with the audience. Typically, brands start using stories to provide a behind the scenes snippets to their followers.

Concentrate On Video Content

Instagram stories are certainly among the best techniques to market your content online. However, don't forget about producing videos along the way. All social networking platforms promote content in the form of videos, and Instagram is not an exception to this rule. Creating content in the form of videos is not difficult, especially because there are various video creation apps which you can use. The popularity of Instagram has given rise to several ancillary applications, which can be used to optimize the benefits provided by Instagram. Hyperlapse and Boomerang are two of the built-in options offered by Instagram, which allow for basic editing of a video within no time. In fact, various brands use these features as part of their video content strategy. The doughnut giant Krispy Kreme uses Boomerang videos and posts them on Instagram.

Instagram is essentially a platform used for promoting and sharing video content. So, don't forget about this essential thing while using Instagram. Videos are a great way to increase your rate of engagement and effectively communicate your brand's message.

The Publishing Frequency

Your publishing frequency is directly correlated to the engagement rate on Instagram. The best way to go about this is by analyzing how often you post and the time at which the content goes live on the platform. Check the frequency of your posting. Spend some time and review your posting history. Do you notice any patterns, or do you have a set schedule? Or do you simply post at random times? Even if your answer is no to both these questions, you don't have to worry about it. By carefully analyzing your brand's Instagram metrics, you can establish the best time for publishing your content and gauge the optimal number of posts you must publish in a week.

Using The Captions Wisely

If you use your captions wisely, you can certainly increase your rate of engagement. Just like the bio, there are a few ways you can use the captions strategically. Don't just think of a caption as a mere description of the post. You can use captions to show off your creative side and also increase engagement. Start including a call-to-action in the captions you post. For instance, you can increase or encourage engagement by asking open-ended, yet polarizing questions in the caption or encourage your audience to share your post by using hashtags or even reposting your content. If you want to trigger any conversations between your followers, then you can include a call to action like "tag a friend" in the caption. You can also use the captions for directing the users toward the link in your bio. When used wisely, not only can you display your brand's personality and voice in the caption, but you can also influence your followers to take action on whatever your call-to-action is.

Use Hashtags

One feature that differentiates Instagram from other platforms is the frequent use of hashtags. Seldom do you see an Instagram post without a hashtag. Every post can include up to 30 different hashtags. A lot of brands don't realize the importance of hashtags. Hashtags serve a dual purpose — they make it easier to search the content you post and also encourage other users to use your brand's hashtags. You can use branded hashtags along with community or generic hashtags. For instance, the reusable red cup that was introduced by Starbucks for the holiday season became widely popular. Starbucks used a combination of custom or branded #redcup along with the common #coffee for promoting its posts. Use the relevant hashtags for increasing the brand's visibility on Instagram.

Start To Repost

You must post content frequently if you want to keep your audience interested. At times, this can be somewhat overwhelming. So, why don't you allow your followers to do some of your work? You can gain new followers and increase engagement by posting user-generated content by using branded hashtags. You can, in turn, repost this content from your profile. When you reshare posts, it makes your audience feel valued, and it also gives you a constant supply of content. The popular shoe brand Vans started curating content by using the #myvans. You can use this tactic whenever you don't have any fresh ideas for posting content or just want to show your followers that their loyalty is appreciated. Reposts are a great way to increase your engagement rate on Instagram.

Thinking Beyond Instagram

It is great that you want to use Instagram for your business. However, are you certain that your existing users, as well as your target audience, are aware that your brand is on Instagram? You might have an incredible social media manager posting brilliant content, but it will do you no good if your audience is unaware of your Instagram presence. This might seem like an obvious thing to consider, but a lot of brands fail to consider this point. For instance, if you have accounts on various social media platforms, then it is a good idea to mention your Instagram profile once in a while on those platforms as well. If your brand has an official page on Facebook, then you can start referring your brand's Instagram pages. Start using social media buttons on your website. You can have their links embedded into your homepage to give the visitor a better idea of all the social media networks you are present on. If you have an existing email list, make a point to refer to your Instagram presence regularly while sending out emails. Apart from this, you can also include a social button in your email list as well.

Active Engagement

You must avoid one of the common mistakes made by a lot of people using Instagram. Instagram is not a platform to establish a monologue. You must not do all the talking but must encourage your audience to participate as well. You cannot engage with your audience if you don't give them a chance to engage with you. The simplest way in which you can engage with others is by replying to any questions and comments posted by other users or even tagging your followers. This not only is a great way of providing customer service, but it also boosts your engagement rate. You must respond to your followers and listen to what they have to say. Don't forget to reply to any mentions your brand gets. Make sure that you respond to the concerns or questions posted by the users as promptly as you can.

Human Touch

Actively engaging with other accounts is a great way to show that your account isn't an automatic bot. In addition to being responsive through comments on your posts or another brand's posts, there are many ways in which you can lend a human touch and humanize your brand's Instagram profile. So many brands are moving further away from just posting promotions about the brands or products and are working on creating people-centric content. You don't have to keep using Instagram as a place for hard selling. Remember, people use Instagram for networking, and if you fail to remember this, you will quickly lose followers. A couple of personal photos here and there and maybe behind-the-scenes snippets can help.

Use Analytics

If you want to improve your reach and your rate of engagement, then you must be aware of the kind of content that clicks with your audience. You must understand what your audience likes and dislikes. To do this, start monitoring your Instagram analytics. Instead of flying blindly and posting without a plan in place by using various analytical tools, it becomes easier to create well-targeted content. The best way to appease the audience is by providing them with content that they will appreciate.

Content Calendar

When it comes to content creation for your Instagram feed, the sky's the limit. You can post customer photos or product photos. You also have the option of choosing videos, selfies, snapshots, and even text overlays. There is no shortage of the type of content you can post on Instagram. If you want to track your posts and increase your Instagram presence, start using a content calendar. A content calendar helps establish a schedule for the content you wish to post. When you know what you have to post and the day and time it needs to be posted, it reduces a lot of your burden. Also, it makes marketing efforts quite easy on Instagram.

The increase in competition, coupled with Instagram's algorithm changes makes it non-negotiable for brands to make certain changes. By using the tips discussed in this section, a brand can optimize its presence on Instagram.

www.ingramcontent.com/pod-product-compliance
Lightning Source LLC
Chambersburg PA
CBHW020919180526
45163CB00007B/2803